Leap of Faith:

How To Build Your Spiritual Business

Colby Rebel

Cover Design: Georgi Petrov

Cover Illustration: Lizzie Martell

Book layout by Logotecture

ISBN: 978-0996653183

ISBN-10: 099665318X

Leap of Faith:

How To Build Your Spiritual Business

Colby Rebel

"Whenever you read a good book, somewhere in the world a door opens to allow in more light." –Vera Nazarian

This book is dedicated to my gram, Jane. You are the bravest, kindest and by far, the smartest lady I know. You are the rock in our family and loved beyond measure. Thank you for always trusting me. You are my inspiration; keep turning the page.

What's Inside:

Part 1: Leap of Faith

Part 2: Business Basics

Part 3: Business Foundation

Part 4: Social Butterfly

Part 5: Terms and Conditions

Acknowledgments

I have no idea how, in just a few short pages, I can properly thank all of the remarkable people who have touched my life and supported me along this journey, but I promise to give it my best effort.

First and foremost, my family
They say you can choose your friends, but not your family. Well, I hit the jackpot with my crew. I am absolutely blessed to have such an incredible family that supports my adventures and encourages my dreams. With every step I've taken, they have gone to extremes to show their love and support for me. *Mom*, thanks for loving me unconditionally. *Love you all.*

My best friend for over 30 years, Renea
Renea has always been by my side with reassurance when I felt discouraged, a pat on the back when I accomplished a goal and guidance when I needed direction. She has seemingly known my true purpose all along. I firmly believe Spirit put her in my life to remind me that I had at least one person in my corner at all times.

My teacher and friend, Lisa Williams
To the teacher, mentor, and friend who helped me expand my own wings and provided a platform for me to fly. Always encouraging me to take the next step, I am forever grateful for the love, guidance, and direction of Lisa Williams. My life forever changed the day she asked me one simple question *"Colby, where's your Master Teacher application?"* Never afraid to give me a push when I felt fearful, Thanks, *Mama Bear*!

My Friends, April and Cindy
There is no way this book would have become a reality if not for the continued support of some very dear friends of mine. April and Cindy continuously encouraged me to write and always nudged me to stay on track. These women have been pillars in my life and provided a safe haven for me to always be myself. *Thank You.*

Tutors
Every teacher guides us. They see your soul and find a way to reach deep within to extract and nurture what is unique within us. Through each of them, you discover a gift that is wonderful. Thank you to Chris Drew, Paul Jacobs, Mavis Pittilla, Jose Gosschalk, and Tony Stockwell.

Fellow Colleagues
So many colleagues have lent their continued support. For every peer who provided insight and proudly stood beside me in this work, thank you for helping me on this path. *Blessed to be among your light.*

Students and Clients
Every student and client has taught me in countless ways to see my own light and strengthen my weaknesses, for each of us is a teacher to one another. I am eternally grateful to have crossed paths with some of the most beautiful and kindest souls on the planet. *Thank you for supporting me.*

My Editors
Let's face it; this book wouldn't be half as grammatically correct if not for the incredible talent of my editing team, Lisa and Daria Anne. Thank you, Daria, for painstakingly going through every word, paragraph and page to ensure that the message I was trying to convey was delivered in the best possible light.

My Grandfather
He came to me at the age of four and asked me to get out of bed to "go tell mommy" what he had just told me. Unaware that he had crossed over a week prior to his visit, I obeyed his request and delivered his message to my mother. Rarely do we receive the gift of validation in such a strong and indisputable way at such a young age.

Spirit
Thank you for never giving up on me. Through every course of action in my life, you were patient, kind, and loving. Through the gentle nudges to the final push, it is with great honor and extreme humbleness that I serve you.

The Round Pegs in the Square Holes
To all who have encouraged me to be the round peg in the square hole – Jen, Michelle, Tracy, Shadonna, Trina and Leanne to name a few of the *very* many -- *Thank YOU*. Your words, actions, and support mean the world to me *Thanks, Rebels.*

All Others
I wish I could name each and every person in my life who has made an impact, but that in itself would take an entire book. From co-workers, employers, fellow master teachers and friends, so many of you have helped me on this journey. I greatly appreciate you. *Thank you from the bottom of my heart.*

Introduction

Many books have been written to help light-
workers develop their spiritual gifts and follow
their life purpose. Very few, however, have
offered a resource to address the practical
aspects of building a solid foundation for a
spiritual business. As I made my transition from
tax manager to medium, it became apparent
that there was a strong yearning from healers
to understand the fundamental business basics
and associated compliance requirements.
Although it would be impossible to include
every intricate aspect needed for business
success, it is my intention to include as many
elements as possible in an effort to create an
all-encompassing resource for anyone
interested in starting their own spiritual
practice.

Throughout this book, you will see the term *company* referred to frequently. Regardless if you are starting out as your individual self, consider this term applicable to you. As you progress through the book, you will see that you *are* your own company. When you can begin to recognize yourself that way, you will emerge with a feeling of confidence knowing you have built a professional business with a solid foundation.

The spiritual community is one that I am incredibly passionate about; I have always been guided to give back by sharing my personal experience, knowledge, and expertise in the areas of taxation and business. Throughout my career, I have personally prepared and reviewed thousands of tax returns that included every possible career imaginable. I have mentally catalogued what makes certain businesses stand out and lead the pack. My knowledge and passion have led to the publication of this book – a book for you, the healer, the practitioner, the visionary and light-worker that sees so much more in the world.

Within these pages, you will discover practical tips designed to help you build a successful spiritual business, one that represents exactly who you are within the industry. This book is not meant to change who you are; it simply gives you the keys to unlock your truest potential and create an outlet that allows you to stand in your own power.

Leap of Faith: How to Build Your Spiritual Business was written with love, compassion, and empathy. I understand the feelings of doubt and uncertainty that come from pushing beyond our natural comfort zone, through my personal experiences; I hope to inspire you to do the same!

"Here's to the crazy ones, the misfits, the REBELS, the troublemakers, the round pegs in the square holes because the people who are crazy enough to think that they can change the world, are the ones who do." **-Steve Jobs**

Part **1**:

LEAP OF FAITH

Chapter **1**

Take Your First Step

Congratulations, Spirit has brought you here! Perhaps you've entertained the idea of doing spiritual work on a full-time basis but are not sure about how to start. This book is your answer. It's a practical reference to help you along your path. From headshots to booking systems and even overall structure, it is dedicated to providing all of the information you need to build your own successful spiritual business, regardless of your area of expertise. Whether your instrument is card readings, crystal healings, reiki sessions, or mediumship, this book applies to any specialty. It is time to spread your wings and take that *Leap of Faith*!

We all know how scary it can be to finally let go and trust, but if you're reading this book; you have been guided by your Spirit team. Know deep within you that you can do this, and that now is your time to shine. Congratulations on taking the next step.

Begin by reading this entire book. I have compiled each chapter to be a bite-sized piece of information, so that after reading, you can use it to create a plan of action for yourself. Intended to assist you with the basics in order to take a step-by-step approach toward building your practice, this book offers easy, detailed chapter titles. You won't have to struggle to find exactly what you need.

As you read, set goals for each day. By setting goals, you are letting the Universe know you are ready for your first step. It may be as simple as jotting down a few ideas after reading a chapter or sitting in a focused meditation on a specific area of the book. By spending time with Spirit envisioning your work, you'll receive inspiration along the way.

Set Daily Goals:

Being productive is a key component to building a successful spiritual business. Think quality over quantity. The best way to be productive is to focus on what matters. It's not about how many tasks you can accomplish in a day; it's about what matters most in moving your business forward. Determine your priorities and make them your starting point.

1. CREATE YOUR LIST

Preparing your list the night before gives you an opportunity to start each day with focus & clarity.

2. PRIORITIZE YOUR PROJECTS

Focus on what matters most. What goal would give you the biggest return on your time investment? This is the where you want to start each morning. Tackle this goal first. When we procrastinate on addressing the most strategic or time-consuming task first, it will only become an energy vampire because it's sitting there in the back of our mind nagging at us to be accomplished. There will always be phone calls, email, and Facebook. Building a successful spiritual business takes self-discipline, so put your best foot forward and you'll walk away with a greater sense of accomplishment!

3. KEEP IT SIMPLE

Not every little chore needs to be on your daily goal list. Just the 2 or 3 main objectives that can really move you forward are the ones you should be listing. You want to concentrate on the quality of the goal, not the quantity of items that can be checked off. If you list too many, you will become overwhelmed and may stall your morning progress because you won't know where to start.

Having clarity on your goals will give you direction. Possessing self-discipline to tackle them will benefit your overall productivity. When you focus on productivity, you achieve results that matter. Results that move you forward. It's all about the *next* step

You don't need all of the answers; you just need to take the next step. Push continuously through any fear you may be experiencing so that you can co-create what Spirit has already manifested for you. As you implement each chapter, you will see your spiritual business forming. Once you begin seeing it take shape, you will start to fully understand what sets you apart and why you are called to be of service.

Chapter 2

Accepting Your Gift

In the beginning, you may have struggled to understand your gift, which you may not have even realized was a gift at all. Most likely, you just knew you were "different." While you may have had "imaginary friends," or dreams or premonitions that came true, no one ever sat you down to explain what was happening. Hopefully, by now you have a better understanding and appreciation for your abilities.

You are a unique individual with a special gift. It's time to own it and step into your calling with confidence. I cannot overstate the importance of believing in yourself because having the assurance to put yourself out there will attract the energy of those in need of your specific healing. Knowing that you are unique and special will keep you motivated when you experience self-doubt. Accepting your gift and embracing your individuality will allow the world to see you in the same light that Spirit does.

Surrendering to your gift may be one of the biggest challenges you face when building a business. Negative self-talk may get in your way, but the more you can stay true to your Higher Self–and listen to that little nudge from Spirit that implores you to keep going, the easier it will be for you to trust.

While building your business, you may encounter self-doubt or skepticism from the outside world. Stay true to you. Don't be afraid to use your voice and commit to what you want. When we resist our path, we will only end up with an uneasy feeling that something isn't quite right in our lives.

Stop for a moment and close your eyes. Take a breath in and release. Now, imagine your life with a thriving spiritual business. You are passionate about helping others, and they are seeking you for guidance and healing. You are experiencing financial security while your soul does its happy dance because it's finally being heard. How does this feel to you? Probably feels pretty amazing, right? The good news is you can absolutely create this as your reality. Let go of worrying about whether or not you're good enough. Let go of needing security to the point that you are sacrificing your potential. If you can trust in Spirit and in you, the Universe will respond.

You are living in a beautiful time of endless possibilities. Entrepreneurship is at its height of acceptance. You have a deep desire to heal and help the world; otherwise, you would not have purchased this book. It's time to accept your gift and move forward by giving your beautiful self and love to the world. Countless people out there need your unique energy and healing, so don't waste any more time!

Chapter **3**

Step Out of the Spiritual Closet

"Never fear shadows, for shadows only mean there is a light shining somewhere nearby." -Oscar Wilde

Now that you've embraced your connection to Spirit, it's time to step out of the spiritual closet. You can't help people if you're too afraid to tell them about your abilities. Some of you may live in smaller towns or suburban areas where this line of work is often looked upon with a skeptical eye. Or, perhaps you come from a background that frowns upon spiritual work. It's time to start looking at yourself as the one who can help change the perception – and in the process, transform lives. Spirit has chosen you to serve, and it is time to live your purpose. If you do this with intention and authenticity, your light will shine. Start believing in yourself and let spirit guide you.

In order to start building a spiritual business, you have to take action. It won't fall into your lap, so stand up, get ready, and step out of the spiritual closet. It is time to tell the world and take a Leap of Faith!

There will be times when you are fearful; please know that this is NORMAL and OK, but you must have the courage to push through it in order to reach your goals. When you have moments of doubt and concern, take a deep breath and surrender. Having the ability to trust your guides and your Higher Self will help immensely when you need to muster up some courage.

When we are challenged, we grow. Each time you try something new or give yourself the permission to step into your path, you are growing. Life is not about becoming stagnant and complacent. It's a journey of self-discovery and a process of building. More than likely, you've been in the spiritual closet for many years. With the door closed, no light can get in or shine out. It's time to turn the knob, open the door, and let your light shine brightly. When you step out of the closet and into your power, your world will become brighter because you are finally embracing your gift and purpose. The only monsters we should fear are the ones we ignore.

Chapter **4**

Making Your Transition

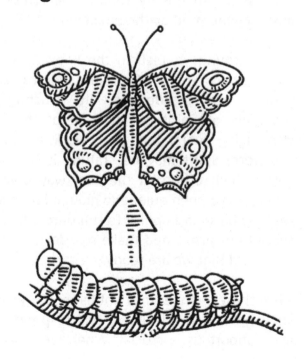

The first rule in transition is practicing patience. Be patient with yourself because your transition may not happen overnight. It takes time. You may be in a position where you are still working a "day job" in which you are bound to an office. No need to allow this to discourage you. You can still build and prepare in a way that creates the best opportunity for a smooth transition into your spiritual practice. There may be times along this journey when Spirit does not "prepare" you and times when you don't always see it coming, but surrendering at each step can greatly reduce the stress and anxiety generated by the unknown.

If you ground yourself in the knowledge that you are fully embraced by Spirit, you can allow yourself the freedom to fly. Trusting the timetable of Spirit can be one of the most challenging feats, but your work is special; therefore, Spirit may be crafting it to enable you to help others in the best way possible. When we've been quiet and hidden for so long, we may have an impulse to run onto a balcony, spread our arms, and make our declaration to the world that we are ready to soar!

Since these changes may not happen overnight, knowing that the Universe will respond to us and support us is crucial. When we make life choices, we shift our energy in a different direction, which means the Universe needs to adjust to match our new vibration. Allowing this book to take you step-by-step into the process of building a successful spiritual practice will prepare you for the change in vibration you will inherently experience, and thus prepare you for the success that is waiting for you.

You will experience many emotions, from joy to doubt. Allow yourself to be present with each one as you continue to trust in your path. You've gotten this far; believe you can do it! Hard work, perseverance, and a desire to serve are the reasons Spirit has chosen you to provide healing to others. Your gift is a beautiful blessing, meant to be shared. Your transition is merely a time capsule and will unfold exactly as it should with each step you take in the direction of your purpose. Be strong and practice self-love, for you are worth it.

Welcome. Your transition has now begun.

Part 2:

BUSINESS BASICS

Chapter 5

Choosing Your Name

Choosing a name can be both exciting and overwhelming. Now that you've finally embarked upon your path, you're eager to step out and own it. You've spent so many years in denial, you want to move forward with authenticity and integrity. This can be a freeing experience. As a result, you may be drawn to calling yourself *Freedom Flies with Fairies*. While this is a great name, it's also important to think LONG TERM.

In your desire to finally share your gift with the world, you may inadvertently limit yourself by choosing a name that creates confusion as your business expands. From using descriptions like "psychic" in your name, to social media and merchant account issues, you may find that in the long term it's best to keep it simple.

Some questions to ask yourself: Who am I? How do I work? Am I an intuitive? A psychic? A medium? Am I an energy healer? Do I utilize a different modality?

It's important to understand the various types of healing so that you can market yourself accordingly. For instance, below are the explanations of intuitive, psychic, and medium so you can see that even areas that may be considered similar are actually quite different.

Intuition: Information comes to you as a flash. These "hits" do not require the application of a logical process because you have the ability to understand it immediately. The information is delivered as it's received. This type of ability is often referred to as "mother's intuition." There is no conscious reasoning behind the information given.

Psychic: Refers to receiving intuition but also connecting using extra sensory perception (ESP). This specialty combines logic and intuition. You may hear the information as your own voice in what is commonly referred to as your *sixth sense.* Psychics will use their ESP to discuss areas of someone's life including love, relationships, finances, family, career, medical or legal. They may even delve into the past, present, and future. There are many belief systems as to how psychics work or should work. This book doesn't explore the various theories; it is merely a reference to give you an idea of how they generally work.

Mediumship: Involves connecting with Spirit with a direct link between Spirit and you, the communicator. It does not entail the use of intuition or psychic ability. Rather, it's a pure link to those on the other side. You may hear it as another's voice. Mediums will generally work with Spirit to provide evidence of that loved one. This evidence may come as a physical description, a crossing, or a personality trait, or in the form of signs and symbols to let their loved one know they are still very much present with them in the land of the living.

If you feel that you are a medium, know that every medium is a psychic, but not every psychic is a medium. You can either choose to market yourself as a psychic medium if you want to offer both or solely as a medium if you prefer to focus on that gift as your primary service.

Perhaps you are an energy healer, animal communicator, palm reader, crystal specialist, or shaman. Regardless of your area of expertise, it's knowing *HOW* you work that matters. *HOW* you work is critical to the way in which you brand yourself. This will be a direct correlation to how consumers will see you in the marketplace.

Be mindful of the words you associate with yourself and your work. For instance, if you choose to use "psychic" in your name, it could be potentially detrimental in terms of advertising, merchant accounts, and public appearances – the reasons for which we will explain later in this chapter.

When you use the word "psychic," you can inadvertently hurt your business, due to the negative stigma some have attached to it. Although the reputations of many industries have been negatively impacted by the bad reputations of some of the individuals who work in them, there seems to be much more attention on the psychic industry. In fact, certain sites and merchant vendors have it listed as a "High Risk" industry. For these reasons, the word "psychic" comes with some potential hurdles.

However, on a positive note, it also states *exactly* what someone can expect from you in regard to your services. So if your specialty is dealing with the past, present, and future, and you want to talk about areas of love, finance, career, health and legal, then, by all means, go out and make your mark in the world by declaring yourself a *psychic*!

Using an alternate name can also create problems with becoming listed in certain directories. Due to past stigmas, the reputations of spiritual light-workers have been challenged. There are several spiritual directories that require applicants to use their "real or legal" names. If you are starting out and call yourself *Freedom Flies with Fairies*, there's a chance you may not be accepted into the directory.

For example, here's an excerpt from renowned Psychic Medium Researcher and Afterlife Investigator Bob Olsen's *Best Psychic Directory* http://www.bestpsychicdirectory.com/pgetlisted.html for submissions:

"REQUIREMENTS TO BE LISTED:

1. *You must use your real FIRST and LAST name (no one-name aliases).*

2. *You must own a website. (You cannot link to a page on a psychic hotline or a social media page.)"*

Another popular directory, Shay Parker's *Best American Psychics,* also requires members to use a legal name. www.bestamericanpsychics.com

Being a part of a directory may be beneficial as it helps potential clients find you. Although there are hundreds of spiritual directories available, choose one that is known for its reputation. For example, *Best American Psychics* tests potential members (twice) prior to accepting them into the directory. This not only helps clients feel secure in choosing a valid directory, but it also reassures you that you are among a league of professionals.

"A professional directory also protects the psychics that are members, as they are assured that the colleagues they are listed with have been vetted as ethical and professional."

-**Shay Parker,** *founder*
Best American Psychics

In today's modern era, there is an increased demand for authentic and legitimate light-workers. There is also a rejuvenated interest in the energy of higher consciousness. People are starting to seek clarity and direction in their lives, and there's an immense desire to find true professionals in the field on whom they can rely and trust. The name you use choose can set you apart and show potential clients you are the real deal.

You want people who seek your services to be able to find you easily. If you are using any other name besides your real name, it may become increasingly difficult for potential clients to connect with you. If you try to pay for any advertising, you will always be advertising for your business name, but you will also have to list your personal name in order to sign up. Consequently, your personal name will always be listed with your business name within the records.

The same scenario can also apply to areas like social media. As an example, let's look at Facebook. You probably already have a personal page, but now that you are starting your business, you will also create a professional page. As you begin working, people will naturally ask you for your name, then search Facebook to locate you. A potential client may find your personal name and try to "friend" you. This creates confusion because the name you created for your business identity does not match the personal profile name.

As your business grows, you may find your private Facebook account flooded with clients and fans, and thus lose the "personal" aspect of your profile. Maintaining one name across the board will help people find the "business" you. It will also help with setting up merchant accounts, becoming listed on directories, and creating an overall ease of finding "YOU" the light-worker.

When you decide upon your business name, you will want to make it consistent across all social media handles. For example, if you are going to use Medium Lucy Leon on Facebook, go for *@mediumlucyleon* on Twitter. Additionally, make sure the name is consistent on other platforms, including Instagram, Snap Chat, Periscope, et al.

Ultimately, you have to commit to whatever name you decide to use. If *you* don't believe in it, it will never *fly.* Creating ease in your branding is one of the crucial first steps in building your brand and creating a successful business.

Now that you have selected your name, it's time to do a proper search to be sure that business name is available. You don't want to go through all the work of setting up your business, only to find that you are unable to use it because there's another medium in the area with the exact same name.

Most states have a secretary of state website that allows you to perform a business name search. You can do a simple internet search to find out the site used in your state or country.

For instance, if you live in California, go to the Secretary of State website, and search Psychic Rebel, this is what you would find: http://kepler.sos.ca.gov/.

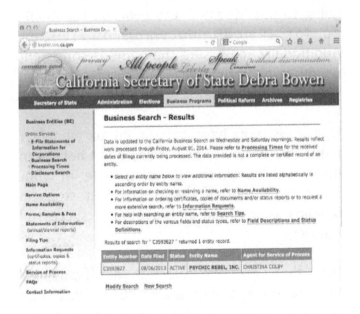

The professional name you choose is a significant part of your work. Whether you use your personal name or decide to be a *Rebel* and go with something different, follow your heart. Following your heart will attract the right clients to you, and lead you to choose a name you will be proud to stand behind.

Chapter **6**

Mastering Your Brand

One of the best ways to figure out your branding is to understand how you are unique to the industry. What sets you apart from the other light-workers? Do you have a special area of expertise? How do you work? What is your personality like when working? Ask yourself, *"Who am I?"*

Having a clear understanding of how you communicate your gift and your presence will be your first indicators of the type of marketing that will work best for you.

Branding is an incredible opportunity to build your identity. Your brand alone will dictate to your client what you represent and give them an opportunity to connect to and communicate with you in a clear and concise manner.

Allow branding to be a reflection of your personality. If you are a soft-spoken person, you may not want a lion as your logo. If you are an extreme extrovert, you may not want a lamb as your logo. See the difference? Think of your brand as your voice.

When your marketing approach matches your personality and your style of work, it will resonate with your clients. They will instinctively sense a genuineness, which builds trust. Clear communication from branding that fits your style will also set you apart because it will focus on your unique characteristics. It will not be lost among thousands of other light-workers in the online search engines.

Most people want to feel connected, so they focus on what makes them alike. This is one area where taking the opposite approach is the golden ticket to building your successful business. Don't be afraid to own who you are and trust that Spirit is working on your behalf to manifest the clients who resonate with you and your message. Like attracts like. When you embrace your uniqueness, you can attract the client who needs your particular healing.

A strong brand helps with referrals. If you have a client who can remember your brand, they are more likely to share it with family and friends, especially if they had a memorable experience. We may forget a name but rarely do we forget a brand that made a lasting impression on us.

Lastly, building your brand should be a fun experience! It's the one area in which you can truly start to figure out how to present yourself and your mission to the world in the most minimal way. Focusing on your branding enables you to determine what you want to say in a few words and colors. Everything beyond that will simply build from that fundamental basis.

"You can build a sustainable business with a good name, but you must have a noticeable brand if you want to leave a lasting impact."

-**Shaun Briggs**, *Graphics, Websites and Branding Expert*

Logo:
Making Your Mark

As previously mentioned, a logo that matches your message can be a game-changer. A logo isn't always necessary, but it can be extremely useful in helping your prospects recognize your business. It may just be your name, a sign, or a symbol, but put the effort into seeing what resonates with you and communicates your style accurately.

Take a moment to write out a few words that either express who you are or the message you want to deliver. Then take those words and associate them with relevant signs or symbols. What colors do you associate with you and your work? Don't choose colors that you "think" work with your field. Go with the ones you connect with on a deeper level. You will have these colors with you for a long time; the more you start from a place of connection, the more your logo colors will resonate with you and your future clients.

Your logo can really communicate the essence of who you are to your community. If we can determine what someone does just by looking at their logo, they have successfully created a strong brand. Our goal is to create a logo that is memorable. It lets our audience know exactly what we do and gives them a sense of how we work.

An effective logo has a few indispensable key components. Incorporating these into your design produces a result that is unforgettable.

1. **Make it SIMPLE.** A complex design will only get lost. Simple designs are not only versatile, but they are easily recognizable.

2. **Let it STAND OUT.** Having a "third eye" to indicate you're a psychic isn't necessarily original or creative. This alone won't set you apart. If you wanted to use the "inner eye" as your logo, design it in such a way that is distinctive.

3. **Avoid STOCK images.** With so many services offering stock images, it's tempting to grab one and use it as your logo, however, since these photos are easily downloadable with one click, they have become increasingly popular and recognizable. It may result in it being recognized as a "stock" photo more than your "company" logo. If possible, find an artist who can design a logo that caters to

you specifically and finds a way to differentiate you.

4. **Keep it TIMELESS.** Fads are fun but can be the pitfall of many companies. A logo that endures over time will resonate for years to come. There may always be small adjustments along the way, but overall, a strong logo won't require a complete overhaul anytime soon.

5. **Factor in COLORS.** When designing your logo, give thought to your color palette. Colors express feelings and can be an unspoken communicator to your message.

Your branding and logo may evolve over time, but the more you can honor your inner voice in the beginning, the more you'll be surprised at how much it still resonates a few years down the road.

As light-workers, we may not want to think about branding; instead, we may want to focus on our message or healing abilities, but it's the branding that will get people to you for that healing in the first place. Don't be afraid to stand out.

You've finally found your calling, now find your voice.

Website:
Your Key to Success

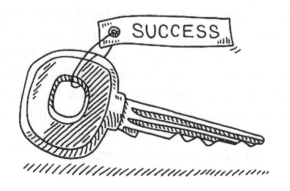

When building your website, it's important to keep in mind that it is a vehicle for telling the world exactly who you are and describing the services you provide. Sometimes when you are starting out, you're thankful to have a paying client! Just remember to think long term.

A website that wanders off in too many directions will confuse your visitors. If someone wants a psychic reading, they are going to look for the best psychic. If your site lists you as a psychic, medium, animal communicator, crystal healer, massage therapist, and whatever various services you decide to include, you will only create a sense of a jack-of-all-trades. This type of site design will limit your potential client base because it's too overwhelming.

Instead, focus on the services your soul really wants you to provide, then express them in a clear, concise way. One that highlights how you conduct your practice as a light-worker. This doesn't mean you can't advertise more than one offering; simply ensure that your website is organized in a manner that's easy for the end user to understand. Your client should be able to pinpoint the service they are paying for when booking an appointment.

In basic terms, you'll want to keep the site clean and minimal. Too much information can create distractions and move the focus away from YOU. Organize and arrange your content in an easily navigable way. Having fewer navigation tabs will produce greater results. What do I mean?

Let's select a topic for the purpose of this discussion: READINGS. Create a READINGS tab with a drop-down menu that features Psychic, Medium, Hybrid, etc. Building a simplistic site that utilizes dropdowns will result in an easy-to-operate experience for your visitors, ultimately leading to more bookings.

In keeping in alignment with overall simplicity, minimize your color palette and avoid the use of too many photos. Of course, *some* photos are important, especially the professional headshot we will discuss in a bit. Including a photo of you on your website is essential to creating a feeling of engagement and trustworthiness with your potential clients.

Don't be shy. Ask clients for testimonials. Having a few testimonials sprinkled throughout your website assures visitors that you have happy clients! It doesn't have to be pages long. In fact, having too many will become distracting, and you'll lose the attention of your visitor. Keeping it focused on a select few will build your credibility and showcase the impact you've had on a client.

If you choose to display videos on your website, which may prove to be a great way to showcase your work, Do NOT have them on automatic play. Although it seems like it would draw them in, keep in mind that they may be at work. Remember that day job we mentioned in the Transition chapter? Speakers that unexpectedly blast sound may actually cause a visitor to abruptly close out of your site. Showing the video in a player provides them with a choice to play it, and if the rest of your website is engaging, will create a desire for them to plug in some earphones and hit "play."

In the end, a well-constructed website will prove to be a huge asset in building a successful, ever-growing spiritual practice.

Business Cards:

First Impressions = Last Impressions

Having a business card is pretty much a requirement. As such, you'll want to invest some money into it because it will be your first impression. If you hand someone a cheap, thinly made card, what is the message they'll take away about your services? It is well worth the added expense to print your information on high-quality paper. I highly recommend consulting with a designer to create cards that match your overall branding in color, fonts, and logos.

Keep it Simple!

Just as with your website, too much information on your business card can lose a potential client's attention and may actually create a sense of less value.

The main information needed for your card is as follows:

- ✓ Name

- ✓ Business Phone Number

- ✓ Email

- ✓ Website

- ✓ One or Two of Your Specialties

- ✓ Logo

- ✓ Social Media Icons (if desired)

Some people feel the need to list all of their services on their card, which can oversaturate your prospect with unnecessary information. Focus on your top one or two services; if you offer more, someone can learn about them by visiting your website – which is why it's always important to include your site address on your business card.

Don't include your headshot on your business card. While it is a common practice in this industry as well as in others such as real estate, honestly, people don't need to see you. Save the space for valuable information that will lead to client bookings.

In an effort to stand out, a popular trend these days is the odd-sized or shaped business card. If you opt for one, you will definitely get kudos for creativity, but be mindful in keeping it practical. If you your card is too small, it may get lost. On the contrary, unless your goal is to have your card to double as a drink coaster, avoid using large round shapes. Designing a distinctive card is vital, but makes a statement for the right reasons. A large business card won't fit into a wallet or business card sleeve. Since it's not practical, it's more likely to get tossed away. Your objective is to create a business card that produces client bookings, not holds cocktails.

When choosing a printer, do your research. Find printing companies with positive reviews from previous clients. If someone hands you a business card you like, don't be afraid to ask them what company they used for printing.

Additionally, you can often visit printers and collect samples of their work, which will help you identify those who can deliver a quality product. Even if given a referral, take the time to review their work firsthand before placing your order, as individual tastes and preferences vary.

There are many self-serve printing services such as Vistaprint and Zazzle. These will certainly get the job done, especially if you are on a tight budget, but since it's do-it-yourself, you are subject to making errors that could end up affecting the final product. A specialized printing company usually provides hands-on customer service through every step of the process – from design, layout, and final printing. Self-serve printing services are a great choice when you can be more flexible with a design or if there's room for some error.

A business card is one of the staples of your business. Invest in quality; it will be well worth the additional cost.

"A well-made professional business card is like a printed good reputation.
Let your business card speak for you."

-**Wendy Wiseman**, *President*
Pixels Digital Imaging

Headshots:

Capturing Your Soul

Wikipedia:
*"A **head shot** or **headshot** is a specific type of portrait (usually a photograph) that realistically demonstrates a person's appearance for branding or casting. Many head shots are promotional pictures of actors,models, authors. Headshots could be a portrait of a face or full body with a background that clearly illustrate the personality inside the person photographed."*

Perhaps one of the single most important aspects to building your spiritual business is your headshot. This will be the main photograph that appears on your website and social media profiles. A common misstep newcomers make is not having a quality headshot on hand. If you've been invited to be a participant in an event or on a show, they commonly request a photograph for promotion. *Please do not make them wait or request it multiple times.*

As the Roman philosopher, Seneca said, "Luck is what happens when preparation meets opportunity."

Being prepared with a professional headshot shows the Universe that you are ready for the opportunities presented to you. Is also reflects your level of professionalism to the outside world and you might just be surprised at how *lucky* you become!

It's vital to get it right. Often, people use a selfie as a headshot. This is a big *NO, NO!* It screams amateur, and you want to exude a feeling of professionalism and competence — one which naturally builds trust with potential clients. Using a selfie sends them a message that you don't have enough money to pay for a professional photographer. It does not resonate a feeling of abundance. You want to naturally build trust with anyone who sees your photo — and you can only achieve that by being natural, authentic, and connected.

Avoid the use of airy and ethereal symbols in your photos: rainbows, orbs, feathers, or clouds. You don't need your hand resting on your chin, a glow placed around your head, or your scarf blowing in the wind. Just be you. Be your natural self. Be *real*. This will make it so much easier for the right clients to find you. Allow your soul to speak through the photo. Trust that your soul is already enough. You may even want to take a few minutes prior to the shoot to meditate and connect to your Highest

Self. Giving yourself permission to be vulnerable in your photo will show your heart. This alone will demonstrate what you are about. Now, that can be scary, but if you're going to do this work professionally, you have to start by showing your cards, so to speak. Let your guard down so that people can connect and trust you.

It's also important to let your personality shine brightly in the photo. Don't try to be something you are not. If you do not naturally smile often, don't display a big cheesy grin in the picture. *It won't look like you*. The same principle applies to the opposite way of being. If you always smile, own that. *Show those pearly whites with confidence.*

Courtesy-Michael Roud, Michael Roud Photography

Choose a photographer with a solid reputation. You want a professional who understands lighting, your goals, and your image; someone who can deliver. Make sure they have a high-quality camera to ensure the photo is focused and in frame, and captures **YOU**. It's understandable that you may not have the funds in the beginning to pay for an acclaimed photographer. If you don't have the money, save up. Perhaps it's as simple as asking Spirit to send you a couple of clients and allocating that money specifically toward your new professional photos. Having photographs that command attention is priceless: invest wisely and plan accordingly.

Consider hiring a professional hair and make-up artist. Whether you are male or female, makeup and hair are crucial to creating a look that brings forth your essence. Consider it this way: you are an expert in guidance and healing, while they are professionals in creating your best look. This is what THEY do. Make-up must be done differently for photos than real life, which is why you want someone who knows how to apply it properly. If you decide on an outdoor shoot rather than a studio shoot, take the weather into account. It may be windy so you will want someone there who can help keep the mane maintained!

You may even want to inquire on the best colors to wear for you shoot. Remember, shades that look fabulous on someone else may not be the most flattering for you. Choose colors that complement your complexion, skin, and undertones.

Be adventurous and try different collar lines to determine what is the most flattering on you. Various necklines include V-neck, turtleneck, scoop, button down, crewneck, etc. Avoid anything too revealing or tight; you want to remain professional. Sometimes the simplest is the most flattering. Busy patterns can be distracting. You want people to see you, not your bright, bold, print floral pattern. Make sure your clothes are clean, ironed, and fresh for the day of the shoot. Planning ahead and ensuring everything is in order will allow you to relax and get a good night's sleep. Remember, proper rest is essential to looking your absolute best!

Deciding on photo re-touching is a personal choice. Some don't believe in retouching, which is completely fine, but again, the angles of a camera don't necessarily capture exactly what the human eye sees. Therefore, some retouching may be helpful in making you appear the way you do in person. Just don't allow anyone to remove all the bags, wrinkles, and lines you've worked so hard in getting. They show who YOU are and represent your experiences. They are *your* story.

If you have these lines of life, and someone removes them all in your photos, you will be unrecognizable when a client meets you in real life. You don't want them to feel as if they've booked with one person, but someone else showed up. It's important to be a true representation of your highest and most authentic self.

Your photo is the window to your soul. It will be the single most effective way to communicate with a client without spoken words. Clients will feel your energy, hear your message and be drawn to you when you let them in. Use your photo as your voice. Allow your spirit to soar and your soul to shine.

"The headshot is a heartfelt look into your soul. It has the potential to make you stand out among and give clients a reason beyond your work to have an intense desire to connect and work with you."

-**Michael Roud**, *Award-winning LA Photographer and Director*

Graphic Design:
Marketing Matters

Marketing yourself is a key component in bringing about awareness of you and your brand. You will need professional banners for your social media accounts and flyers when you start to hold live events. In addition, marketing tools such as pamphlets and business cards are also helpful as they are easy to hand out during a conversation.

When it's time to start creating your banners, flyers, and other materials, you will want to utilize the service of a professional graphic designer. Having professional materials reflects thought and care in yourself and your work. Clients really respect this, and they know that if you cared enough to create such beautiful marketing tools, that you put thought into your work all around.

Let's say you want to hire an interior designer for your house. You go to two different designers and their place of business.

Designer #1 has a space that is in disarray. The samples are strewn about the room, the walls have peeling wallpaper, and it looks as if it hasn't been remodeled since 1977.

You now visit designer #2. This designer has all of the samples neatly arranged by color, texture, and manufacturer on shelves. The walls are freshly painted, and artwork is hanging to add color and depth. Just based on this information, which designer do you feel would produce the best results for your remodel?

The above case does not define WHICH of the two is the more qualified designer, yet based on the above example, we intuitively have a feeling that designer #2 cares about their work and will do the work better. That's how clients see light-workers.

Putting thought and care into your work will reflect positively in your business.

Building a business does not just take a natural gift. It takes professionalism, business savvy and a sense of care about the image and brand you are putting out to the world. When you do create social media banners, it's helpful to incorporate your colors with your logo. The more you can tie them into your marketing materials the easier it will be for clients to recognize you.

Sometimes we can feel that if we promote ourselves too much, we are working from ego, but it's the opposite. If you are concerned about putting yourself out there, you are working from little ego. The little self, that somehow you are not enough, or you are bothering others by putting yourself out there.

This is your time to embrace your service to spirit. If you are reading this book, you are ready to SERVE and work at your fullest potential so there's no need to be shy! Share yourself and your materials, time to let the world know you are READY!

"Dealing with a creative designer is the best route when it comes to creating your branding, logo or any promotional materials. They will guide you, give you good advice, listen to your feedback and most important, make sure you are 100% satisfied with your final product.

Give to the creative a small drop of water and he/she will turn it into an ocean, give them a flower and they will turn it to a beautiful countryside field, give them your idea and they will turn it to successful and memorable design."

-**Georgi Petrov**, *Founder & Lead Designer*
Designroom1229 and Flyer Room.

Chapter 7

Securing a Business Line

Business Telephone

When you first started doing client sessions, they were probably friends or acquaintances, correct? You just wanted to see if this whole "gift" thing was "real." Well, here you are now, so you can trust that YES, it is "real!"

Now is the time to get a proper business phone number. Using your personal cell number to conduct business is not only unprofessional; it will eventually become an *energy vampire*. As you build your business, you must set boundaries. No pun intended, but you will need to have the ability to disconnect. If your business is tied to your personal cell phone, you'll deprive yourself of the all-too-critical down time necessary to recharge your spiritual battery. Like your cell, you will get drained easily and run out of juice.

If you want to be taken seriously as a professional, then you must create a professional environment. One in which you have a designated business line, with an outgoing message informing your clients and potential clients that you will return their calls within 24-48 hours. People will respect this *and* actually perceive it to be of *better* quality. Please do not text your clients! Offering them the ability to text you will create a breeding ground for panic situations, emergency sessions, and last-minute cancellations – all of which creates a vibration of desperation. Avoid this outcome by deciding how you want to work and the kind of energy you want to call into your practice.

There are professional services offered at minimal cost that will give you the freedom and professionalism to help you shine in your industry. Companies such as *FreedomVoice* can give you a business number that will allow you to take the calls directly or have them routed to an alternate number. All of the calls are still at your fingertips, but you will have an extra shield of privacy for your protection. If you miss a call, and the caller leaves a message, it will go to your email. This way, you will have the opportunity to check the message at your leisure.

Many landline phone services are inexpensive these days. As you can see, there are plenty of options available to give you the professional edge and the downtime you need to create the best client experience possible.

As you grow and expand, you may need to consider hiring an assistant who can handle the calls on your behalf. You will have to train someone to answer the phone and the client questions in a way that adheres to your policies. Trust that the effort will pay for itself as it frees up valuable time you can use to focus on building your business and conducting spiritual sessions. While this option may seem to exist in the distant future, just keep it in mind as a gentle reminder when your business is booming! Freedom Voice: https://goo.gl/9maUTm

Business Email

The days of using your personal email account for business are over! Setting up separate business email accounts is an absolute must in creating a sense of professionalism. Business email provides added layers and boundaries to your practice. Having at least two separate email accounts for your business is recommended. One address would be for your direct contact colby@colbyrebel.com, and the other would be for general inquiries such as info@colbyrebel.com.

When giving out your business contact information, you would provide the info@colbyrebel.com address. This avoids an expectation that you will personally respond to every email query. Although you may be eager to personally reply to each and every email, it becomes more difficult and time-consuming as you grow your practice. If you start your business by answering clients personally, then at some point tell them you've become "too busy," it may create a feeling of you not caring. If you begin your business with these practices in place, it becomes full disclosure as to how your business operates and avoids any surprises to your clients down the road.

Consider hiring your imaginary friend! Personally responding to every inquiry can be time-consuming and energetically draining, but when you are starting out, you may not have other feasible options. One idea is to create an imaginary assistant. You set up an email address under that person's name; for instance, kendal@colbyrebel.com. This gives you an option to reply as that person. Your imaginary friends have always been there with you so consider hiring one of them to respond to your emails!

Chapter 8

Utilizing a Booking System

Another wonderful tool is a solid online booking system. Providing a system that allows clients to book directly can vastly increase your revenue. It can turn potential visitors into paying customers. An online system provides potential clients with 24-hour access to your availability. And since most systems offer a visual calendar as part of their features, they give clients an opportunity to choose a day/time that works best for their schedule.

Take the time needed to research various online booking systems as each one offers its own unique and varied elements. You have to find the one that best fits your needs. If you are not the most tech-savvy individual, a simpler system might be the best for you. Others allow for complete customization with coupons, discounts, color-coding, etc. If you know your way around code, these can give your booking system a completely integrated feeling within your website and add a nice aesthetic value.

You always have the option to hire a professional to help with the coding, but as your business evolves and expands, you may need to understand how to make simple changes to your booking system without having to rely on your IT web developer. Making the changes yourself will save you time and money, as well as expedite the updates.

As mentioned in Chapter 6, you want to limit the amount of services available on the booking system. Consolidate where you can.

Having too many options will leave the novice client unsure of what type of session is best for them. This may lead to more questions than answers. Write down all of your services. Determine which ones can be placed in groups. Whether by time or service, you will see that there is a way to simply what you offer. You can also create questionnaires or memo sections so that a client can provide any particular detail you desire.

For instance, let's say you offer psychic and medium sessions and a hybrid of both. There's no need to create three different services. Create one 60-minute reading session, and then offer a questionnaire that allows them to select between psychic, medium or hybrid. Making your system as simple and easy-to-use as possible is the key to success.

With an online system, you will have the option to select business hours, days, or specific appointments. In the beginning, you may be tempted to be as accessible as possible, but refrain from leaving your calendar open 7 days a week, 24 hours a day. A limited supply of availability will help give the impression that you are busy – and being busy creates demand. Another great advantage of an online booking system is the opportunity to up-sell. For instance, if you offer gift certificates, you can list them directly on your website as an option for those looking for that unique gift. Same holds true for other items such as packages and products. Creating ease in any transaction will certainly help "seal the deal" and manifest greater returns for your business. Another utilization of an online booking system is to offer discount codes. They can serve as an incentive in capturing a visitor's attention, thus serving as a catalyst in influencing them to finalize a booking.

For example, you could offer a "first time" code for any new client looking to book a session with you. This serves as a great invite as people love to feel as if they are getting something of value at a discount.

Perhaps, aside from convenience, one of the best features of an online system is instant payment. Most booking systems partner with credit merchants to offer direct payments. Whether PayPal, Square or another provider, allowing a client the convenience and ease of scheduling and paying immediately will surely result in more bookings.

Some systems offer social media integration or can link to your mass email service providers. This can create a significant impact on building the all too important client email list.

Here are a few booking systems that offer various levels of service.

www.acuityscheduling.com
https://bookedin.com
http://www.vcita.com
http://www.supersaas.com
https://www.genbook.com
http://www.appointy.com
http://www.fullslate.com

Keep your appointments!

Another important aspect of a working spiritual professional is being timely with your appointments. Maintaining a high level of commitment and professionalism with appointments will help establish your reputation – and a strong reputation is the key in a service-driven industry.

Clear communication is also imperative for appointments. One suggestion is to create an automatic email to send to your clients once they book the appointment, along with a follow-up reminder 24 hours in advance.

The email should remind them of the following:

✓ Date of appointment

✓ Time of appointment

✓ Type of session booked

✓ Cancellation policy

✓ Company policy for late appointments or "no shows"

✓ Contact information

In regard to client policy, you may want to make sure the client is held responsible for their appointment. If you allow for last minute cancellations, you can be sure that's the exact type of client you will attract. Of course, unexpected events come up, but limiting the amount of exceptions and "bending" the rules will help you maintain your boundaries. By allowing one client to arrive late, yet still giving them the entire session, you will create a domino effect, resulting in subsequent appointments being late. That may upset or inconvenience those clients who have honored their commitments. It's important to respect your clients' time as you never know what they had to go through to make time for the appointment with you in the first place.

Showing respect for your time will ultimately reflect as showing respect for your clients' time as well. If a client is late, and they lose 15 minutes of their session, you can guarantee that next time they will be on time. However, if you extend the session, it only gives them permission to be late in the future since you have been so accommodating.

Having an online booking system and being timely with appointments will set you apart from your counterparts in the industry. The booking system will allow clients to schedule at their leisure. If they are visiting your website at 11:00 p.m., they don't need to worry about reaching you personally for an appointment. They can book their appointment, make the payment, and receive their confirmation all within a few key strokes.

Not only does this make it more convenient for the client and give them a sense of instant gratification, but it will also give you more time. Time to invest in areas that will help your spiritual business grow!

Chapter **9**

About ME – Writing Your BIO

Now that you have a professional headshot and a structured website, it's time to work on your bio. Yes, I'm referring to that *ABOUT ME* tab! As a spiritual light-worker, it may be difficult for you to talk about yourself. While you may feel that it's your ego talking and not you, look at it as any other business. If you're seeking to hire someone to perform a service for you, wouldn't you want to know a bit about them before hiring them? Wouldn't you want to see that your doctor or lawyer is licensed? You would want to know how long your tax accountant has been in practice, right? The same principle applies to you and your business: it's OK to OWN who you are and be proud about it.

The best bios combine a bit of experience, training, and personality. It does not need to be an entire resume, nor does it need to list your five kids, three divorces, and ten cats. Having a well-rounded bio will reflect YOU. For example, if you have worked with some prestigious teachers, you'll want to include a bit of your training. However, if you've only taken a two-hour workshop with Lisa Williams, do not describe yourself as someone who "trained with world-renowned Lisa Williams." Such a statement would be misleading. Be honest. If you don't have any training, you may want to consider taking classes. Doing so not only builds your confidence, it helps you expand your network.

Start your bio off with a bit about how you work. What makes you different? What do you have to offer in the reading that sets you apart? Then, briefly explain your philosophy. How do you see things? Next, mention a bit of your training, awards or accomplishments.

Finally, end it with something personal. Do you like gardening? Enjoy reading? Riding Unicorns? Whatever the case may be, including a sentence or two about your interests reminds readers that you are a real person.

A well-rounded bio can attract clients on its own. You don't want it to look like a grammar school fill-in. Be original and share the information you would want to know if YOU were seeking the services of a spiritual professional.

Chapter 10
Safety Awareness

This is perhaps the single most important area to trust your intuition. As spiritual beings, we can sometimes overlook the practical side of remaining safe. Taking precautions is a necessary part of your practice. Gender is irrelevant as we can all fall victim to a predator. This chapter is not intended to instill fear by any means, but to help you become aware of all aspects of having your own business. With just a few tips and reminders, you can raise your safety awareness.

Working from Home

You may think working from home is the ideal situation. However, there are drawbacks that should be considered. Not only are you inviting a variety of energy into your personal space, you are also welcoming an innumerable amount of strangers. Once they step into your home, they will have intimate details to the layout, access and security. You never know what type of situation you may encounter. For instance, consider the girl who is trying to break away from an abusive relationship and comes to you for guidance; or you've crossed paths with someone who becomes infatuated with you. Both are very realistic situations and by taking reasonable precautions, we can create boundaries that help us remain safe at all times.

Of course, we want to believe and hold the intention that only those working for the highest good are led to us, but incorporating safety measures should be part of your business modality.

If you intend to see clients in your home, create an area exclusive to your work and partition off the rest of the house. Restrict the client from having access to all other areas by keeping bedroom doors, hallways, etc. off limits. Since a restroom is probably needed, choose one that is closest to your dedicated work area. Even if you are fortunate enough to have a room exclusive to sessions, you still want to keep the remainder of the house as private as possible. Perhaps keeping a TV or radio playing softly in one of the rooms might help give the impression that someone else is in the house with you just for an added layer of comfort.

I also recommend investing in an installed security system. Today's modern systems typically come with panic keys or buttons which may be critical in the event of an emergency. It can't hurt to have a small can of pepper spray close by as well. We certainly don't ever want to be in a situation where we have to resort to these measures, but personal safety is a top priority. Creating and managing a successful business means thinking of everything and doing your best to be prepared.

Commercial Location

If your practice is held in a commercial location, be mindful of your office hours. If you see clients in the evening, choose a location that isn't too remote and offers ample outdoor lighting. Remember that during certain months it tends to get darker much earlier, which means even a 5:00 p.m. session could be nightfall.

Upon leaving the office, be aware of your surroundings. Don't allow devices such as cell phones to distract you. Keep your head up and eyes peeled to your environment. These simple, small actions can dissuade someone who may have had ill intentions.

Dealing with a Stalker

It's hard to imagine that you would have to consider how to handle an obsessive client, but it does occasionally occur. In this business, clients can become so enamored by your work that they become infatuated with being part of your energy, healing, and vibration. Adversely, it may lead to them having a desire to be part of your life in an unhealthy way.

When you receive unsolicited or uninvited contact with someone on a repeated basis that creates a feeling of fear or distress, there's a possibility you are encountering stalking behavior. This could vary from harassment and threats, to gifts and adoration.

Examples of common behavior exhibited by stalkers:

- ✓ Excessive telephone calls & emails

- ✓ Unsolicited gifts

- ✓ Excessive monitoring on Social Media

- ✓ Unwarranted text messages

- ✓ Visits to home/workplace without an appointment

- ✓ Uninvited contact

In many areas, stalking is considered a criminal offense so you may have legal recourse, if necessary. However, when the menacing actions come from a client, your inner empath may be hesitant to accuse them of stalking. I remind you: your *safety* is your *priority*. If you encounter improper behavior, reach out for help and contact the proper authorities.

Self Defense

We may be lovers and not fighters by nature, but having a few self-defense moves up your sleeve certainly can't hurt should you encounter an unexpected situation. Giving yourself every opportunity to defend yourself is your right. Knowing a simple block, punch or kicking technique may just give you a better chance at keeping yourself safe!

Perhaps the most important safety measure is to trust your intuition. If you are NOT feeling comfortable, END THE SESSION IMMEDIATELY. Do not worry about feeling bad if the client hasn't necessary "done" anything. Your intuition is always right so trust it and listen to it.

Part **3**:

BUSINESS FOUNDATION

A strong structure is the foundation of a successful business. When you work in the healing arts with the intention of helping others, it can seem overwhelming to deal with the business side of the industry. Some of the information below may be a little confusing at first, but take the time to read it through a few times so that you can get a grasp on the business types.

As much as you may want to run out and just start seeing clients, laying a solid foundation is a necessary component. You want to create a structure that allows you to build and grow from a place of strength while helping you to maximize your true potential. It may take some self-discipline to learn about basic business structures and bookkeeping, but doing so will help you thrive in doing what you love to do.

The first question to ask yourself is, *what type of business do I want to be?* Each type of business structure has its pros and cons. Think long term. You may not want to jump into something immediately, but at least choose options that provide you with flexibility for future growth.

Chapter 11
Choosing a Business Type

Without a doubt, this will be one of the most important decisions you make as you embark upon your spiritual practice. Keep in mind, you do have options, some of which can be changed as your business grows; in the meantime, here are the most popular business types to consider. I highly recommend seeking legal and accounting counsel since your specific circumstances may impact the entity type that would be most beneficial to you.

You may have the best of intentions; however, seeking out a professional, certified tax preparer or attorney is truly the best way to go. This is their field of expertise. You wouldn't want a doctor giving you a reading, right? So why are you trying to do your own taxes? Just put it out to the Universe that you will do an extra session or two to cover the cost of a professional tax preparer. Not only will this ease your stress, but your tax advisor will be able to ensure you are filing in compliance and getting the most out of it.

Having certified and licensed professionals advise you on the proper set up could save you in the long run. When you're starting out, it can be tough to fund all of the start-up costs, but doing it right from the beginning can only save you time and frustration in the future.

Sole-Proprietorship

A sole-proprietorship is considered by many to be the most basic of all entity types. This is usually referred to as a Schedule C and is reported directly on your personal tax return. As the individual, you own and operate the business and have total control over reporting. You will report all income and expenses, then report the net income on your personal tax return. You are also responsible for all taxes and any liabilities that are derived from the business.

When it comes to a business name, you have a choice: you can either use your personal name, or you can create a DBA (doing business as) with a different one. For instance, if your name is Sharon Light but you like to call yourself *Eternal Lights,* then you can either have the business name as your own, or you can create a DBA and use only the *Eternal Lights* as the name. If you decide to use the DBA, you must also file a fictitious business name statement with the proper authority where your principal place of business is located.

The sole proprietorship may be a good choice if you want the most control and flexibility over your business and decision-making. It's less expensive to maintain and requires less overall record keeping. However, although not always the case, the Schedule C does tend to have a higher audit risk and there is no liability protection; hence you are personally held liable. So you'll have to consider the pros and cons when making your decision.

LLC: Limited Liability Company

There are two main types of LLC's. The first is a Single Member LLC (SMLLC), where it is only yourself and you decide to set up your business as a Limited Liability Company. This business type is disregarded for Federal tax purposes; so ultimately, it's very similar to the sole-proprietorship as mentioned above. It is reported directly on your personal tax return as a Schedule C. As a result, we will skip over this one and move forward to an LLC that has more than one member.

An LLC that has more than one member will file its own tax return. It becomes its own separate entity. You will also file for an EIN, but you will now file this tax return as a form 1065. Each partner will receive a form called a K-1 and that form will be filed with your personal tax return.

LLC's tend to be flexible, but it's highly recommended to have an operating agreement. An operating agreement dictates the conduct of the business, and the general affairs and resolution of the entity. Even if your spouse or a best friend, you still want to have an agreement that clearly communicates what happens in the event of a disagreement or dissolution. Although it's never anticipated disagreements will arise, it's important to protect yourself and your business in the event it should occur.

LLC's may also have an annual fee; please check with your secretary of state to see if applies to where you live. There is generally an additional fee for the tax preparation since it's recommended to use a professional CPA to prepare the tax return.

One positive aspect of an LLC: if you are not in a position to start your business off as an S corporation, you can have it initially established as an LLC and then convert the status to an S-Corp at a later date by filing the proper paperwork. If you think this may be a part of your future, include language in the operating agreement that will also be relevant to an S-corporation shareholder agreement (see below). If you include a set of bylaws, this would also work as a shareholder agreement if prepared properly. This stresses the importance of having the entity set up properly from the initial filing.

Please, I implore you, find a good attorney and tax accountant who can advise you and help you get it all started.

S-Corporation

An S-corporation is its own entity, separate from the shareholders (owners). The entity pays its own tax and files its own tax return; the shareholders receive a K-1 that is then reported on their individual personal tax return. The shareholders are then taxed on their K-1 reportable income. To form an S-corporation, an *Articles of Incorporation* must be filed with the appropriate secretary of state. One of the benefits of an S-corporation is the ability to pay the officers a salary which is deductible from the company profits. This can be a significant tax advantage if your business expands significantly. As with the LLC, an S-Corp should have a shareholder's agreement in place prior to the start of business. This agreement will reduce confusion and help to avoid any activities that may terminate the "S" Corp status. There is a rule referred to as "piercing the corporate veil." For example, if a shareholder is conducting activities that are not within the guidelines of the S-corporation (such as making personal purchases with the company credit card) it can be perceived as piercing the corporate veil, potentially jeopardizing the entity as a whole. Putting in place the shareholder agreement will clearly define the expectations and guidelines permissible within the corporation as a whole and by the shareholders individually.

If you do have a partner with your S-corporation, you may want to consider adding an indemnity clause within the agreement. This will help protect the entity and other shareholders. It basically states that if a shareholder does do something that jeopardizes the S-Corp status or termination of the corporation, that the partner responsible will pay the financial consequences.

"Your choice of entity really is the foundation on which you will build your business. Give it some thought and learn the advantages and disadvantages of each type. Even if you decide to start with a Sole Proprietorship, have a plan for the future for if and when you will use a more formal entity. Unexpectedly changing direction mid-stream can not only be expensive, but will also distract you from running the business, right at the time the business probably needs your attention the most!"

-**Jamie Cottage**, *CPA, President*
Cottage & Associates, Inc.

Leap of Faith

Form SS-4
(Rev January 2010)
Department of the Treasury
Internal Revenue Service

Application for Employer Identification Number
(For use by employers, corporations, partnerships, trusts, estates, churches, government agencies, Indian tribal entities, certain individuals, and others.)
► See separate instructions for each line. ► Keep a copy for your records.

OMB No. 1545-0003

EIN

T Y P E	1	Legal name of entity (or individual) for whom the EIN is being requested

TYPE OR PRINT CLEARLY

2 Trade name of business (if different from name on line 1)

3 Executor, administrator, trustee, "care of" name

4a Mailing address (room, apartment, suite number, and street, or P.O. box)

5a Street address (if different) (Do not enter a P.O. box)

4b City (if foreign, see instructions) State ZIP Code

5b City (if foreign, see instructions) State ZIP Code

6 County and state where principal business is located

7a Name of responsible party

7b SSN, ITIN, or EIN

8a Is this application for a limited liability company (LLC) (or a foreign equivalent)? ☐ Yes ☐ No
8b If 8a is "Yes," enter the number of LLC members
8c If 8a is "Yes," was the LLC organized in the United States? ☐ Yes ☐ No

9a Type of entity (check only one box). Caution. If 8a is "Yes," see the instructions for the correct box to check.
☐ Sole proprietor (SSN)
☐ Partnership
☐ Corporation (enter form number to be filed) ►
☐ Personal service corporation
☐ Church or church-controlled organization
☐ Other nonprofit organization (specify) ►
☐ Other (specify) ►
☐ Estate (SSN of decedent)
☐ Plan administrator (TIN)
☐ Trust (TIN of grantor)
☐ National Guard ☐ State/local government
☐ Farmers' cooperative ☐ Federal government/military
☐ REMIC ☐ Indian tribal governments/enterprises
Group Exemption Number (GEN) if any ►

9b If a corporation, name the state or foreign country (if applicable) where incorporated State Foreign country

10 Reason for applying (check only one box)
☐ Started new business (specify type) ►
☐ Hired employees (Check the box and see line 13.)
☐ Compliance with IRS withholding regulations
☐ Other (specify) ►
☐ Banking purpose (specify purpose) ►
☐ Changed type of organization (specify new type) ►
☐ Purchased going business
☐ Created a trust (specify type) ►
☐ Created a pension plan (specify type) ►

11 Date business started or acquired (month, day, year). See instructions.
12 Closing month of accounting year

13 Highest number of employees expected in the next 12 months (enter -0- if none). If no employees expected, skip line 14. Agricultural Household Other

14 If you expect your employment tax liability to be $1,000 or less in a full calendar year and want to file Form 944 annually instead of Forms 941 quarterly, check here. (Your employment tax liability generally will be $1,000 or less if you expect to pay $4,000 or less in total wages.) If you do not check this box, you must file Form 941 for every quarter ☐

15 First date wages or annuities were paid (month, day, year). Note: If applicant is a withholding agent, enter date income will first be paid to nonresident alien (month, day, year)

16 Check one box that best describes the principal activity of your business.
☐ Construction ☐ Rental & leasing ☐ Transportation & warehousing
☐ Real estate ☐ Manufacturing ☐ Finance & insurance
☐ Health care & social assistance ☐ Wholesale-agent/broker
☐ Accommodation & food service ☐ Wholesale-other ☐ Retail
☐ Other (specify)

17 Indicate principal line of merchandise sold, specific construction work done, products produced, or services provided.

18 Has the applicant entity shown on line 1 ever applied for and received an EIN? ☐ Yes ☐ No
If "Yes," enter previous EIN here ►

Third Party Designee
Complete this section only if you want to authorize the named individual to receive the entity's EIN and answer questions about the completion of this form.
Designee's name
Address and ZIP code
Designee's telephone number (include area code)
Designee's fax number (include area code)

Under penalties of perjury, I declare that I have examined this application, and to the best of my knowledge and belief, it is true, correct, and complete.
Name and title (type or print clearly) ►
Applicant's telephone number (include area code)
Applicant's fax number (include area code)

Signature ► Date ►

BAA For Privacy Act and Paperwork Reduction Act Notice, see separate instructions. FDIZ2901 01/30/10 Form SS-4 (Rev 1-2010)

C-Corporation

Like the S-corporation, the C-corporation is its own entity; however, there is one significant difference. The C-corporation pays tax separately, and no K-1's are issued to owners. This type of corporation does not usually work with a service-based industry, but check with your lawyer or accountant for any special exemptions that may apply to you.

Factoring in the benefits and drawbacks of each entity type to determine which one fits best into your current needs, as well as considering future needs, will help you choose the most appropriate entity from the onset. This reduces the risk for error as you grow. The LLC, S-Corporation, and C-Corporation will limit your liability, but require the most compliance. The sole-proprietorship is an easy start-up with minimal filing but does not offer liability protection.

Consult with your legal counsel and tax attorney or accountant to evaluate your personal circumstances to find your best overall fit.

Obtaining an EIN

An EIN is a Federal Employer Identification Number. This is NOT a Social Security Number, but a separate number assigned to your business by filing the IRS form SS-4 (Application for Employer Identification Number). Commonly referred to as an EIN, it is helpful to have, as it can keep your personal security number private.

Even if you use your personal name as your business name, you can still apply for an EIN to help provide a level of personal identity protection to your business.

You can apply for an EIN directly online by visiting:
https://www.irs.gov/businesses/small-businesses-self-employed/apply-for-an-employer-identification-number-ein-online

Business Tax Registration

Determining your state and local tax obligations is also a component to establishing your business. Most states have various imposed taxes that require registration and annual filing. For instance, some states require a business tax registration. In some areas, this is referred to as a *City Business Tax* and is based on the "right to do business" in that particular area. Contacting the business licensing sector of the city in which you plan to operate will help inform you of the filing requirements pertaining to your specific area.

Below is a sample of a city business tax certificate from City of Los Angeles, CA.

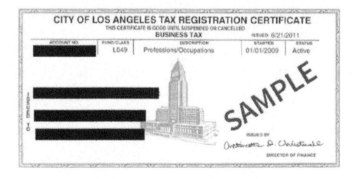

Chapter **12**

Bookkeeping and Basics

As an entrepreneur, wouldn't it be wonderful if you didn't have to worry about logistics? Sorry to break the news to you, but in order to build a successful spiritual business, it is necessary to understand a bit about bookkeeping, financial reporting, and filing requirements. This may be the most "un fun" part of it all, especially when you have a desire to simply heal others and provide your service at the highest level.

However, the more you learn about the back-end of your business, the more power you will have to create one that is financially abundant and in compliance with the laws and regulations of your area.

Understanding the financial aspect of your spiritual practice will give you the ability to make important decisions that directly impact your success. Many entrepreneurs do not realize the value of learning and comprehending how their business works. As a result, they are held at the mercy of advisors, accountants and others professionals who may or may not make decisions in the best interest of their client, *you*. This is your business. YOU have the opportunity to learn EVERY aspect of it. By doing so, you will be able to create a successful and expansive spiritual business!

Learning the bookkeeping basics will give you the tools needed to help you build. You can track what areas are not profitable and create a forecast that will assist you in creating growth year after year.

If you're new to finance and accounting, consider taking a beginner's bookkeeping class to help you learn the basics. There are so many classes at your disposal designed to assist the novice. If you have a busy schedule or live in a remote area, you can easily locate one online. When searching for a class, find one that feels informative and covers the reporting procedures for your specific region.

When it comes to complying with IRS regulations, bookkeeping basics are essential. You must understand the items that should be reported as income and those you can expense. If you have set up an S-corporation as described in a previous chapter, it is particularly important since you want to be mindful not to "pierce the corporate veil" which we will discuss further in the next chapter.

Even if you don't choose an S-corporation, knowing what you can and cannot deduct is the taxpayer's responsibility, not the accountant's. Knowledge of your company will not only help you manage your business better, it will give you a sense of empowerment.

Understanding financial statements and how they work can get extremely complex. For the purposes of this book, we have left them as simplified as possible and directed the information that would most generally suit you in order to help you understand the basics.

If you're new to finance and accounting, take this chapter slow. You may have to read it a few times, but it will also provide for a quick reference later if you get stuck!

Cash vs. Accrual

There are two primary methods of record keeping and accounting that indicate how you track your business's income and expenses: cash basis and accrual basis. Although in a service driven industry, the cash method is more commonly used, I will provide an explanation here on both methods.

✓ Cash Method (cash basis)

Record all payments upon receipt and deduct all expenses when incurred. Income won't be considered earned until it is received. So promises of payment or invoicing won't count as income until you physically receive the payment. The expenses are deducted when you pay them. If you pay with a credit card, the expenses are deductible per the date of the transaction, not the date the credit card payment is made. If you use your credit card for expenses in the month of December, yet don't pay that credit card until January, the expenses are still deductible in the month of December.

For example:

You have a client that emails you for a session. You send them an invoice of $150 to reserve the booking. That fee is not considered income until they pay the invoice. If you have the session in January but the client pays in March, you will include it as income in the month of March. When the payment was actually received.

✓ **Accrual Method** (accrual basis)

Under the accrual method, you record income when the service is ordered or rendered, regardless of when the payment is actually received. Expenses are deductible when you receive the goods or services, not when you physically pay for them.

Using the same example as before, a client receives a reading in January, yet did not pay until March. The income would be recorded in the month of January when the service was rendered. If you incur an expense, it becomes deductible when the service is completed, or the goods are received (and installed-if necessary).

As first mentioned, in a service driven industry the cash method is more common. It's also a simpler accounting method to maintain.

Now, **WHEN** you become extremely successful and earn over **$5** million a year, or you have over **$1** million a year in inventory (goods you sell), you are required to adopt the accrual method of accounting. Looking at the bright side, if you are grossing over $5 million then you will definitely be in a position to hire a bookkeeper to help with the record keeping!

Having a grasp on the cash vs. accrual method provides you with an advantage to understanding your overall business accounting system.

Income Statement (Profit & Loss)

An income statement is also referred to as a profit and loss. The terms are generally interchangeable. This is a financial report that summarizes your operations. This includes your income and your expenses. When you take the revenue (earnings) and then subtract your operating and administrative expenses, it results in what is referred to as net income. The net income is an indicator as to whether or not your income exceeds your expenses or vice-versa.

There are a few main components of an income statement: revenue, cost of goods, gross profit, operating expenses, and net income. There are others, but these are the major players; the ones most relevant to a service-based industry.

Revenue

Revenue is the amount earned either by a service provided or a product sold.

Cost of Goods (Purchases)

Cost of Sales or sometimes referred to as purchases is the cost of goods or services provided. For example, you sell bath salts that have been charged with crystal healing. In cost of sales, you would include the purchase price of the jar, the salts, the crystal, any oils to provide fragrance and packaging. These are your cost of goods.

These would be listed in a separate section in your accounting software aside from normal operating expenses. Tracking these expenses will help you determine the overall profitability of a product. It can be extremely useful when needing to make a decision about discontinuing a product or in finding ways to lessen your costs to create the product so that the product can be more profitable.

Gross Profit

Gross Profit is your revenue less the total of cost of goods. Revenue-Cost of Goods=Gross profit. This figure represents a profit (or loss) before factoring in your general and administrative costs.

Operating Expenses

Operating Expenses are the expenses needed to run the business as a whole. These expenses include selling expenses, general and administrative expenses. There are specific examples of operating expenses in the next pages, but a few include: *Advertising*, *Rent*, *Telephone*, *Salary Expense*, etc.

Net Income

Net Income is the total revenue less the cost of goods and the operational expenses. Your net income is the final amount that indicates your profit or loss from your business.

If you set up your business in an accounting software program (discussed later) it will usually have the capability of generating this report. When the data is input into the program properly, the report can be very detailed, specific and accurate. This report is very helpful when filing your tax return as you can simply hand this report to your accountant and they will be able to use the information directly from the report.

Not only is an income statement helpful for ease of tax preparation, but it can be an extremely useful tool in tracking the profitability of your business. Software systems even allow for a month by month or year by year comparison so you can track your success!

Sample Income Statement:

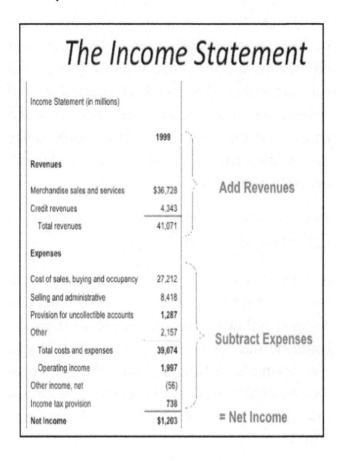

Balance Sheet

A balance sheet is a financial statement that outlines a company's assets, liabilities and equity at a specific point in time. If you are a sole proprietor, then think of yourself as the "company". The balance sheet lets someone know what the company owns in assets, owes as liabilities and the amount invested by the owner/shareholder.

The formula for a balance sheet is Assets = Liabilities + Shareholders' Equity.

A balance sheet is a financial snapshot at a specific moment in time. It indicates a company's financial health since it can show if a company has debt, assets, and equity. If you are looking for a business loan, the bank may require a balance sheet to show whether or not the company has value, pays its bills and has equity.

Let's break down which each of those means in the real world!

Assets

Assets are the resources a company has that lends to either current operations or future economic benefit. Assets are normally easily convertible to cash and are considered to have liquidity. Examples of assets are cash, machinery and equipment, furniture, fixtures, buildings and land. There are several others types of assets, but these are the primary ones most likely utilized by a spiritual business.

Some examples of assets:

Cash is the most liquid of all assets. This would be a business checking or savings account. Any account holding cash or cash equivalent under the company name would be considered an asset (unless it holds a negative balance, i.e. an overdrawn account).

Equipment that is owned by a company and has a life of greater than a year is also considered an asset. Examples of equipment are computers, cameras, recording equipment, and vehicles.

Buildings and Land can be a valuable asset. If you have a building you own and conduct your business from this location, it would be considered an asset. The same holds true for land. An example would be an office building. If you lease the office building, this would not be considered an asset. You must *own* the building in the company name.

Liabilities

Liabilities are debts that the company owes. For example, let's say you took out a business loan to build your business. This would be considered a debt until paid off. Debts can include sales tax payable, taxes payable, salaries payable, or accounts payable. If you purchased jars for salts and the vendor lets you pay over time, the portion that you still owe would be listed as a payable on the balance sheet.

Equity

Equity is the net investment you have in your company after accounting for liabilities. The basic formula for equity is:

Capital - Withdrawals +/- Net Income.

Reporting Income

You may currently accept cash as a form of payment. Regardless of the payment method, all income received for services or products is reportable income. It's best to be honest, so if a client pays you cash, you should report it. No matter how large or small the amount of payment may be, reporting it properly is required. If you receive a cash payment, deposit it into your business account. Then, if you have an expense, pay it from that business account.

A paper trail is important for several reasons. If you are ever audited, you will need to verify and prove your income and expenses. The IRS will review bank statements and look closely at any cash deposits. They may reconcile the total to your income tax return filed.

When you continuously use cash, it can make the tracking more difficult because it's easy to misplace a receipt or even forget that you took the cash payment and purchased groceries with it. An online payment system will allow you to be more organized and enable you to build a business plan from the financial information you're tracking.

With electronic payment systems like PayPal and Square, it's convenient and easy to accept these forms of payment, thus alieving yourself of any worry about properly reporting your income. These merchants will provide you with a report at year-end detailing the total receipts received for the year. If you also use a booking system as mentioned in the previous chapter, they may also include reports to help you track your income.

Lastly, we will examine some bookkeeping software that can also be used to report your income and expenses.

Tracking expenses

If you want to determine how well your business is doing, you must take your total income and subtract your expenses. This is called your net income. Net income is how you want to determine your overall profitability and growth. It's not determined solely by your income, because if your expenses increase, you will actually earn less overall. When launching a new business, you can anticipate incurring a significant amount of initial costs. You may have start-up costs associated with legal expenses, filing fees, business cards, marketing materials, and perhaps deposits if you plan on having a commercial space.

You may be wondering what type of expenses qualify for your business? Well, they can vary, but I've compiled some general examples to help you. Feel free to print out the handy chart, which you can complete and submit to your tax preparer. In order to deduct the expense, it must be related to the business. It must be what is considered ordinary and necessary. An ordinary expense is something that is common within your industry.

For example, Tarot cards would be considered common in the spiritual industry because they are tools used on behalf of clients. A necessary expense would include rent for the commercial space in which you operate your business. Below are some of the most common expenses. Remember the rule: they must apply to your business and be ordinary and necessary to qualify.

Advertising: This applies to any advertising you do, including Facebook, Google AdWords, or Yelp. Any service you pay for to help market your services would be a deduction to consider.

Bank Charges*:* Having a separate business bank account is recommended to track your income accurately and ensure that you are not co-mingling personal with business income and expenses. A business bank account normally incurs costs like a monthly service fee and an initial set-up fee. Both would be deductible for your business.

Business Cards: The expense of hiring a company to produce, print, and design your business cards is also considered a business expense.

Commissions: Do you pay someone a commission to help you book sessions? If so, this commission you paid out for the generation of business can be expensed.

Gifts: If you buy a client or colleague a gift, it can be expensed; however, the IRS threshold is $25 per person.

Legal and Professional: Here's some good news. You know that accountant and lawyer we recommended you hire to help set up your business? Well, the amount you paid to them is deductible! That added benefit may just be the inspiration you needed to hear to heed my advice.

Postage expense: The cost of postage purchased for mailings or such associated with your business can be expensed.

Printing: Did you have flyers printed? Pamphlets? The cost of printing for business can also be expensed.

Professional dues: If you pay professional dues for directory memberships or professional associations directly related to your business, you can expense them. A word of caution: it is usually not acceptable to deduct gym memberships and such by claiming they are for business.

Seminars and Trade Shows: Did you pay to be a part of a fair? Or attended fairs for business? In the spiritual industry, there are countless events and expos. The costs associated with these can be deducted if incurred for your business.

Telephone: The cost of a having a professional business line can be expensed. Even the business portion of your cell phone can expensed, just don't deduct the whole amount unless you never use your cell phone for personal use.

Other Expenses:
Computer & Internet Fees
Insurance
Licenses
Materials and Supplies
Office Expenses
Publications
Samples & promotional items

Leap of Faith: General Business Expense Record Sheet

Operating Expenses	Cost of Goods Sold
Accounting Expenses	Product Purchases
Advertising	Materials & Supplies
Bank Charges	Cost of Labor
Business Cards	Other:
Brochures/Pamphlets	Other:
Cleaning & Maintentance	Inventory at beginning of year:
Commissions	Inventory at end of year:
Computer & Internet Expense	
Dues & Subscriptions	
Gifts	**Equipment**
Insurance	
Legal Fees	Computer Purchase
Office Expense	Furniture & Fixture
Postage	Machinery & Equipment
Printing Expense	
Professional Dues	
Rent Expense (Office)	
Rent Expense (Other)	
Repairs	
Seminars/Booth Expense	
Supplies	
Taxes & Licenses	
Telephone (Business Portion)	
Other:	

*The purpose of this worksheet is to assist you in organizing your tax-deductible business expenses. In order for an expense to be considered for business, it must be both *ordinary and *necessary expense. Do not include personal expenses, reimbursed expenses or expenses that are anticipated to be reimbursed.

Organize your expenses

Please, whatever you do, do not hand your tax accountant a shoe box full of receipts! In fact, don't give them *any* receipts. Your accountant does not need to see or hold onto your receipts. Instead, keep an Excel spreadsheet that lists your expense categories and simply provide the totals. Most tax preparers bill the same way that lawyers do: on the time incurred.

If they have to go through to categorize and total your receipts, you're guaranteed it will increase the time spent on your return and more than likely, result in a higher tax bill. As your business expands you can always seek the help of a bookkeeper and an easy-to-use accounting software program, but for the novice, the Excel spreadsheet is a quick, organized and easy solution.

Create a filing system

Create your own personal filing system, starting at the beginning of the year. Simply purchase a portable filing box or *Pendaflex*-style organizer and label each tab with an expense category. For instance, office expenses, supplies, advertising, et al. As you accumulate the receipts, simply put them in the matching category. At the end of the year, you now have all of your receipts ready to go – no searching for them necessary!

You then total the receipts in each category, then list them on the Excel spreadsheet you created in step 1. Not only will you impress your accountant, but you will also feel a sense of ease not having to worry about finding and sorting a years' worth of receipts all at once. After each category is totaled and your tax return is complete, take your receipts and put them in envelopes and label the expense on the front. Store the envelopes in a box and put them in a safe place. You'll generally want to keep them for a minimum of three years for IRS purposes.

Do you need a bookkeeper?

Keeping yourself organized in the financial department is a necessity to building a successful business. If you start off and don't have this area organized, it will only become more stressful and overwhelming as you grow. It's better to get it right from the outset. With that being said, it may not be within your financial budget to hire a professional bookkeeper initially. Don't let this discourage you as there are plenty of options available to assist you in compiling your information into a beneficial system.

As mentioned earlier, you could create an Excel spreadsheet to track your income and expenses. This will be the most rudimentary and least expensive option. It's also open to errors and mistakes as it will take your due diligence to keep it updated properly. Still, if you're just starting out and lean on finances, this may be a perfect solution for you.

Another option is to purchase accounting software. A couple of them are fairly simple to understand and user-friendly. QuickBooks and Quicken are two of the most popular programs available. You can even take one of their training courses and hire one of their certified experts to help you set it up properly.

If you're more of a do-it-yourselfer, *how to* videos are available. Thinking long term, this would be your best option. You can maintain the accounting yourself and at the end of the year simply print the necessary reports for your tax accountant. The software also has the ability to generate reports for creating a budget.

Although a bookkeeping software program is not as user-friendly to the novice as an Excel spreadsheet, the extra investment more than pays for itself once you take the time to learn the program. In a few years, after you've become madly successful, you can then hire a bookkeeper to maintain the accounting without needing to re-create it all. Intuit is the manufacturer of QuickBooks and Quicken. Gather more information by visiting: http://quickbooks.intuit.com or http://www.quicken.com

Issuing 1099's

The IRS 1099-MISC is a reporting form that informs the Internal Revenue Service that an independent contractor has received at least $600 in taxable income. When utilizing the services of an independent contractor within your trade or business and you pay them at least $600 within a calendar year, you may be required to issue a 1099-MISC to them. These payments only pertain to those derived for the purpose of your trade or business, thus personal expenses are not applicable. Examples of services would be web designer, assistant, accountant, legal services, consulting, sales commission, etc.

Services paid to a corporation do not need to be reported on a 1099.

Upon engaging someone in services, request that they complete a form W-9. This form captures their name, Tax ID and address. This will save a lot of time and frustration at the end of the year when trying to compile the data to

complete the 1099's. People relocate or refuse to provide their social security or FEIN so having it prior to the first payment issued alleviates the potential issue altogether. Here is a copy of the form W-9. You can download this form and keep it for future use.
https://www.irs.gov/pub/irs-pdf/fw9.pdf

The IRS has a right to impose penalties for those who fail to report and file 1099's. If it's found that the negligence was intentional, the penalty is significantly increased.

Reviewing your records at the end of the year with your tax accountant can help reduce the risk of oversight.

"Having a basic understanding of bookkeeping and maintaining proper financials are the most critical success factors for any business. Keeping a clear picture of your company's financial health will enable you to evaluate your business' weaknesses and strengths; bringing you one step closer to manifesting future profit."

-Allen H. Park, CPA, MBT, Partner
Apark Accountancy

Here is a sample of a 1099-Misc

		CORRECTED (if checked)	

PAYER'S name, street address, city or town, state or province, country, ZIP or foreign postal code, and telephone no.	1 Rents $	OMB No. 1545-0115	Miscellaneous Income
Mesages from Heaven, Inc. 1111 Spirit Crossing Hwy. Angel City, CA 91122	2 Royalties $	**2016** Form 1099-MISC	
	3 Other income $	4 Federal income tax withheld $	Copy B For Recipient

PAYER'S federal identification number	RECIPIENT'S identification number	5 Fishing boat proceeds $	6 Medical and health care payments $	
33-1122444	111-22-3333	7 Nonemployee compensation $ 777.00	8 Substitute payments in lieu of dividends or interest $	This is important tax information and is being furnished to the Internal Revenue Service. If you are required to file a return, a negligence penalty or other sanction may be imposed on you if this income is taxable and the IRS determines that it has not been reported.
RECIPIENT'S name Lucy A. Lightworker 11 Surrender Avenue New Purpose, CA 91122		9 Payer made direct sales of $5,000 or more of consumer products to a buyer (recipient) for resale ▶ ☐	10 Crop insurance proceeds $	
		11	12	

Account number (see instructions)	FATCA filing requirement ☐	13 Excess golden parachute payments $	14 Gross proceeds paid to an attorney $	
15a Section 409A deferrals $	15b Section 409A income $	16 State tax withheld $ $	17 State/Payer's state no.	18 State income $ $

Form **1099-MISC**   (keep for your records)   www.irs.gov/form1099misc   Department of the Treasury - Internal Revenue Service

DO NOT FILE

Personal Expenses

As a general rule, you cannot deduct personal, living, or family expenses. If an expense is partially related to the business, you can deduct the business portion, but not the total amount incurred. For instance, if you have a cell phone and use part of it for business, determine the amount that would be considered business and deduct that portion.

Let's say you have a total cell phone bill of $200. You determine that 60% of your cellular phone use is for business use. You would then deduct $120 on your business records, and the remaining $80 would not be deductible. It can get a bit tricky to apply this formula so it's highly recommended to keep any business expenses as separate from your personal expenses as much as possible.

As tempting as it is to write off the massage, the gym membership, and the wardrobe, it's just not advisable. It's quite difficult in an audit to get the IRS agree to those expenses, even if you claim medical purposes. So just consider them as personal health and well-being items and stick to reporting those that are truly related to your business.

Being stringent about refraining from deducting personal expenses is even more important if you own a corporation. As previously mentioned, habitually attempting to write-off personal expenses under the guise of business may put you in jeopardy of *"piercing the corporate veil."*

Exercising discipline with the allocation of expenses will help you maintain organized records. Having the few extra dollars in write-offs isn't worth the stress of worrying about whether or not they would be accepted under the scrutiny of an IRS review.

Opening a Business Account

After you've chosen a business name, decided on the business structure, and obtained a FEIN, you'll be ready to open your business bank account. Having a business bank account separate from your personal bank account is crucial. You want to start off on the right foot by reporting your business income independently from your personal income. This not only sets clear, definitive boundaries on what is personal versus what is business, it will also keep your business income organized by segregating and tracking that income.

And it creates ease in reconciling your account activity each month because you will be able to tie a bank statement to the accounting software program, thus ensuring you don't miss any deposits or expenses. Maintaining accurate financial reporting is fundamental in building a business plan and conducting accurate financial reporting.

Choose a bank that offers the most benefits and simplicity of operations. You will need your IRS confirmation that your business was assigned a FEIN. If you are a corporation, you will need your Articles of Incorporation and a valid ID. Check with your specific bank to see if they require anything additional, but those are the general basics needed to open an account.

Having a business checking account requires some self-discipline. You will want to refrain from making personal purchases from this account and accurately report any income derived from your business. The more precise you can be about reporting business income and expenses from the business account, the more reliable your financial reporting will be. This will be a time-saver at the end of the year when you are required to compile all of your information to either issue 1099 forms, prepare for your year-end tax projection, or forecast for the next year.

At first, it may take some practice, but once you get in the habit of only using this one account for all of your business needs, it will become second-nature.

You can also use business checks to pay for any services or fees allocated specifically for your spiritual practice. If you use this option, get into the habit of writing the details of the purchase in the memo section. You'll be glad you did at the end of the year as it will help you immensely.

For your business account, you can pay any qualified business expense including inventory, professional fees, business rent, or advertising. In Chapter 12, we will discuss various business expenses that qualify for payment directly from your business bank account.

Most banks will charge a monthly service fee. This is a deductible business expense you can write off at the end of the year against your revenue.

Opening and operating a business bank account will establish you as a professional and create a clear intention of a "for profit" business.

Chapter 13
Other Considerations

Office in Home

Working from home can be a blessing; it can also be a tax deduction! However, you want to be certain that you qualify for the home office deduction since the IRS has strict rules about this. There are two basic requirements by the IRS for home office deduction. The first is that the home office must be a space used exclusively for conducting business. If you keep your treadmill in your office and spend time working out to your favorite TV program, it won't be considered exclusive to your business. Secondly, you must be able to prove it's the principle place of business. One exception is that you may be able to deduct it if it's a separate structure or space, like a garage, studio or even a barn if this is not-your principle location for business.

The possibility of a deduction is fantastic news if you have a home office or a space designated for clients (in that case, you may be able to deduct the portion that is designated solely for business). These expenses include mortgage interest, real estate taxes, utilities, repairs, insurance, and depreciation. The computation for calculating the deduction is based on total square footage of the property and then the specific area dedicated to business.

For example, if you have a 1,500 sq. ft. house and 250 sq. foot is your business office, then 16.66% would be considered deductible for business purposes. There is a second method called the simplified method. In this method, you would take the business square footage – the 250 sq. foot and multiply that by the $5, the prescribed rate (this is the current allowable rate). Your deduction under the simplified method would be $1,250. The calculation would be done on a specific tax form called an 8829.

Deducting your home can be a potential audit red flag so you'll want to keep records and be confident in the business use prior to taking the deduction. To learn more about office in home and its requirements, review https://www.irs.gov/uac/about-publication-587 and check with your tax accountant for further assistance in determining your eligibility.

Auto Expense

If you drive your car for business, you may be able to deduct the business portion of use. There are currently *two* methods allowed by the IRS to make this determination: the standard mileage rate and the actual expense method.

Standard Mileage Rate Method

Each year, the IRS determines the rate per mile permissible. Under the standard mileage rate, you take the current year allowance per mile and multiply that by your total business miles driven. You can check IRS publication 463 https://www.irs.gov/pub/irs-pdf/p463.pdf for the most up to date information regarding the current allowance.

For 2019, the mileage rate is .58 cents/mile. If you drove a total of 12,000 miles in 2019 and 5,400 were for business, then you are permitted a deduction of $3,132 for auto use. For the mileage rate, all mileage driven must be documented. Purchasing an auto log is a great way to maintain your mileage. There are also software programs that can also help you track and store the business mileage driven. One site that offers mileage tracking is TripLog: https://triplogmileage.com/IRS-Uber-tax-deduction.html

Below is a sample mileage log that would be needed to help track business mileage for deduction purposes.

Table 5-2. Daily Business Mileage and Expense Log   Name:

| Date | Destination (City, Town, or Area) | Business Purpose | Odometer Readings | | Miles this trip | Expenses | |
			Start	Stop		Type (Gas, oil, tolls, etc.)	Amount
	Weekly Total						
Total Year-to-Date							

You can also purchase mileage log books from most office supply stores such as Office Depot or Staples.

Actual Expense Method

The second method of choice for deducting your business portion of auto is the actual car expense. In this method, you would take the total miles driven and divide that by the business miles. This gives you a business percentage. You then take your actual expenses. Some examples are as follows:

Registration Fees	Garage Rent	Repairs
Maintenance	Tires	Depreciation
Lease Payments	Fuel	Insurance

*Parking fines are *not* deductible!

You would then multiply these amounts by the business percentage calculated previously to give you the actual dollar amount available for deductions.

Whether you use the standard mileage method or the actual expense method, having accurate and detailed record keeping is essential. Per the IRS, proof should be kept in a log book, online tracking app, expense sheets or an account book. Keeping receipts and canceled checks are a great way to provide evidence if the expenses are ever challenged by the IRS.

Keeping your records

It is generally recommended that you keep your receipts and records that support your deductions for three years from the date the return is filed with the IRS (including extensions).

Meals & Entertainment

Your daily caffeine fix may feel necessary to you, but it may not be considered tax deductible. For a business and/or entertainment expense to qualify as a business expense it must meet the following requirements:

✓ Main purpose of the expense was active conduct of business

✓ You engaged in business with another person

✓ There was an expectation of deriving income or business benefit at some point in the future.

Unfortunately, the IRS does not consider all entertainment expenses to be created equal. Some specific entertainment expenses are *NOT* deductible, including: country clubs, golf clubs, gym memberships, airline clubs and hotel clubs.

Business meals are generally deductible at 50% by meeting the following rules:

✓ Directly related to the active conduct of your business

✓ Not "lavish or extravagant"

✓ Either you or an employee must be present at the meal

By adhering to the requirements above, incurring meals and entertainment expense with a genuine intent to conduct active business and generate income will generally prove to be deductible. Keeping your receipts and jotting the detail on them is beneficial in supporting your claim as a business expense.

Travel

Bon Voyage! Did you know you may be able to deduct your business travel? When certain requirements are met, your business travel may be considered a deduction.

1. BUSINESS RELATED:

The travel must be primarily for business purposes. Recreational or vacation travel is never deductible. Travel must be in the pursuit of an existing business.

[?] You may not deduct travel that is associated with the pursuit or acquisition of a business. The business must already be in existence. If

you do incur costs to acquire a business,
they would be added to your start-up
expenditures.

*No family allowed! Having a spouse or dependent
join you on the trip may seem like a great idea, but
you are not allowed to deduct their travel unless
they are employees of your company. For a spouse's
travel to be deductible it must also be classified as a
"bona fide" business expense.*

2. ORDINARY AND NECESSARY:

In order to deduct travel expenses, they
cannot be lavish or extravagant. They must
be ordinary and necessary to your existing
business.

3. MIXING BUSINESS WITH PLEASURE:

What do you do if you have a trip that is
partly for business and partly for pleasure?
The rules state that the trip must be
primarily for business. If your travel is
primarily for pleasure, you may **NOT** deduct
ANY portion of the travel. However, if the
trip is primarily for business, then you
would be required to allocate the expenses

and deduct the portion that is related directly to your business.

4. NO STAYCATION:

For travel expenses to be valid, your travel must be away from the general proximity of your principal place of business.

Please contact your accountant or tax attorney for unique situations as special rules apply to having more than one place of business, no place of business, or temporary assignments.

Below is a list of the most common expenses permissible based upon compliance and circumstances:

- ✓ Lodging expense
- ✓ Airfare fees
- ✓ Local travel: Taxi, Bus, Rental Car, Train
- ✓ Cleaning & Laundry expense
- ✓ Business Telephone/Fax expense
- ✓ Meals (generally 50%)
- ✓ Tips paid on business related expenses

- ✓ Other expenses directly related to the travel in the ordinary course of conducting business

Sell products?

Do you sell physical products? Perhaps candles, crystals, tarot cards or unicorns? If you sell any tangible items, you will need to file for a seller's permit through your state board of equalization.

The requirements to hold a seller's permit generally applies to the following:

- ✓ Individuals
- ✓ LLC'S (both single-member and multi-member)
- ✓ Partnerships
- ✓ S-Corporations
- ✓ Corporations

Seller permits apply to both wholesalers (you sell to other businesses) and retailers (you sell to the public)

You can do a quick search to locate your specific agency. Generally, you can apply directly online. Your accountant should also be able to assist you with this if you are unsure how to complete the form. Once you register, you will be given an account number; then it is your responsibility to collect any sales tax on behalf of your state for the taxable products you sell.

A sales and use tax return would be filed with the calculated sales tax paid upon filing. Based on your anticipated sales, the board will determine if you are a monthly, quarterly or annual filer. This would be the frequency of the filing of your returns and the payment submitted. Be sure to collect the sales tax and, if possible, hold it in a separate account since the state sees you as an agent on their behalf. For this reason, you want to always have the funds available.

You will also want to notify the agency if you should change any of the following:

- ✓ Change of business physical or mailing address

- ✓ Discontinue your business

- ✓ Sell your business

- ✓ Change the name of your business

- ✓ Change of email address (for online filing)

Audits

What is an audit?

An audit is a review or examination of financial reporting to ensure compliance was met, and the information was reported accurately per tax laws. An audit can be done by various agencies and for a multitude of reasons. For example, an audit may be performed on a tax return filed, payroll reporting or sales and use tax, just to name a few. Most tax agencies have the authority to perform examinations.

Examinations occur when a taxing authority chooses to validate income, deductions, and overall proper reporting.

Although it would be impossible to dictate exactly what triggers an audit, there are a few reasons that stand out as "red" flags.

Below are a few reasons why a return might be selected for an examination.

1. **INCOME NOT DISCLOSED:**

Income earned is reportable. Taxing authorities such as the IRS, State agencies, and local agencies will reconcile your income to that reported to them directly. If you receive a 1099 or a W-2, the IRS receives copies and may hold you accountable for the income not disclosed.

2. **FILING A SCHEDULE C:**

As discussed in Chapter 11 a sole-proprietorship has the potential to trigger an audit, especially when reporting a loss. If there are a few years' worth of losses, the IRS may classify your business as a "hobby" and disallow the loss on your tax return. Generally speaking, the IRS likes to see a profit 2 out of 5 years. This may be more difficult when starting a business because losses are more common at the outset. This is one of the reasons maintaining accurate financial records and keeping receipts is important. The documentation supports your position and can help with producing a favorable outcome upon examination.

3. HOME OFFICE:

Deducting the home office can be a common audit trigger. In a spiritual business, it's very common to utilize your home office for services, but remembering to follow the guidelines will help to support your expense.

4. AUTO USE:

Reporting excessive auto use or multiple autos can also be considered a red flag. Unless you have a delivery truck for business, claiming 100% of your car will certainly raise some eyebrows.

5. **TRAVEL & ENTERTAINMENT:**

Abuse in any category can draw unwanted attention to your return. This is particularly relevant when reporting travel, meals, and entertainment. If you have too many write-offs, you may unknowingly be creating an audit trigger.

6. **CASH BUSINESS:**

If you operate a business in which you primarily take cash as payment, you may unwittingly trigger an audit. This is a high alert for the IRS as cash business tend to under report so they perform examinations to ensure all income is being reported properly.

If you incur the expenses legitimately and maintain accurate records to defend your claims, there's no need to refrain from taking these deductions simply because they tend to be "red" flags. Being prepared and having the ability to justify your position is essential in securing a favorable outcome in the event they are examined.

Part 4:

SOCIAL BUTTERFLY

Chapter *14*

Building Your Platform

Once upon a time, social media wasn't a factor in business success, but those days are long gone. With instant gratification becoming more of a sport than a past time, you must allow yourself to be visible to potential clients. Not only visible but reachable. If they can't see you, they can't find you. If they can't find you, they can't book with you.

Creating your brand on social media can draw an audience to you. The benefits of social media are nearly endless – not only in revealing your services to the public, but in giving them a glimpse of your style and personality. Across your social media platforms, consistency is critical – from logo and branding to communication.

Why is it important? You want potential clients to truly get a sense of who you are. Avoid mixed messages; instead, attract the right client type to you in the shortest period of time. For example, if you want to specialize in animal communication, focus your branding, images, and communication around that specialty to create connections with those who have a desire for that particular service.

Don't be afraid to allow your personality to shine through. Each individual soul is our fingerprint to working with Spirit. Therefore, embrace who you are and how you work, especially on social media platforms. The more authentic you can be, the more freedom you'll have to interact and create a community that supports your work.

Reach out and ask people to support your social media pages. From LIKES to subscriptions to the sharing of posts, the more you can put yourself out there to the public, the quicker you can build your spiritual business. Be creative with your approach. Offer a contest or a discount to those who support you and your work. Nothing builds a business quicker than a client who feels appreciated!

Facebook

Facebook is the #1 social media platform, with over 1.62 billion users currently. If you think of it in terms of an audience, it's a pretty massive one for your message! Facebook is a social media platform that allows you to post photos, create events, list your business, and promote yourself in a way that gives you exposure to those outside of your immediate geographical location.

Most of us already have a personal Facebook page, but for your business, you'll want to set up a separate professional, public page. This will allow you a level of privacy and give you an opportunity to engage other users on a professional level. You can post contest, events, media and videos. Taking some time to think about the message you want to share will help you target your public profile. Who are you looking to reach? Who will benefit from your style?

Facebook even offers an option to advertise or boost certain posts. While this is a great feature, there are several rules you must abide by in order to get your post approved. Before spending the time, money, and effort to boost the post, read through the guidelines to ensure your ad will be approved. It can be incredibly frustrating to create an ad, only have it disapproved within a few hours of posting. When that happens, Facebook stops boosting it immediately. You can learn more about Facebook's policies right here: https://www.facebook.com/policies/ads/.

One of the most common ad mistakes is when they contain over 20% text versus image. When you are creating an event, class or workshop, you want the information on the flyer. Yet, when it comes to Facebook, you won't have the luxury of unlimited text. So try to structure ads that focus solely on the necessities. There are programs and apps that will allow you to run the ad through it to see if it meets the 20% text/image rule. If the ad you created does have text that exceeds 20%, Facebook may allow it to run temporarily due to its new rules, but will eventually disapprove the ad, and it will stop running.

Some believe the ads don't help because they are not seen by every follower or friend you have. However, if you create target groups and focus on your specific audience, Facebook ads can be beneficial. In the beginning, you may have a strict budget; be creative and find other ways to promote your events. Send it to friends and ask them to share it. Find Facebook groups that permit posting on their page and submit your upcoming activities that way. It's ok to start small and build. This will give you an opportunity to see what is working and not working for your brand. Be creative in finding alternate ways of getting your message out there!

Twitter

With 1.3 billion registered users, twitter is definitely a contender in the social media ring. It works differently from Facebook in that it allows for little mini messages. The current format is 140 characters, which means your information needs to be short, concise, and engaging. It does let you post photos and videos, but if your aim is to share photos, you may find Instagram (which will be addressed later) more suitable.

Twitter lets people know what you're doing in this instant. With twitter, you don't need to be accepted as a "friend." You can simply follow anyone — including celebrities, light-workers, philosophers, etc. — see their tweets, and become engaged in their content.

This is the mission statement directly from Twitter:

"Our mission: To give everyone the power to create and share ideas and information instantly, without barriers."

When you create your twitter profile, you will want it to be similar to your other social media profiles so that anyone who is looking for you can find you easily. In fact, using the same photo across social media platforms is a great way to build immediate recognition.

Twitter is a great platform for staying current in the world, whether microblogging messages from Spirit or informing followers where they can find you. It's a great networking tool if you can configure your messages to its format.

When you use Twitter, you want to create a strategy that will help engage your current followers and attract new ones. The best way to this? Remain authentic and genuine to you.

Keep your tweets short. Remember, it's 140 characters, so if you try and express too many things, it will not seem focused. You can always link back to a longer blog or article, but to create an impact on the tweet, keep it short.

A photo can enhance a tweet's impact. If it's visually stimulating, it will draw in followers and engage them. This is exactly the result you are striving for on your social media platforms: #Engagement.

Don't be afraid of being personal. Allow yourself to shine through your tweets and engage with people in a way that they can feel connected to you. It doesn't mean that you can't keep some of your life private, but when you can show them a bit of your personality, share your insights, or interact on an intimate level, you will create loyalty among your followers.

Instagram

With 100 billion monthly users, Instagram is a fun social media platform! It basically allows you to tell a story through a photo. Unique photos that show a slice of life seem to do exceptionally well on Instagram, from nature to cooking to selfies. Allowing the outside world to view an authentic moment of real life builds engagement with your audience. Instagram is a wonderful tool to help you in branding yourself as well.

Take something that's personal and passionate to you, and then find photos that relate to it. Let's say it's Siberian Huskies: find cute pics of huskies and post them. Over time, people will associate huskies with you; however, this activity also offers a personal touch by giving people an opportunity to peek inside your life.

Focus on a mission statement for Instagram. What will be your purpose, your mission with this particular social media tool? Write it out so that it's concrete and you can refer back to it when needed. As with every other platform, you need to create a strategy with Instagram.

Answer the following in writing:

1. **What is your *message*?** What do *YOU* want to say to the world?

2. Now, who are you delivering that message to? **Who is your target *audience*?** These are the people you want to reach with your message.

3. What are you hoping to achieve? Do you want to drive more traffic to your *website*? **Want to build *followers*?**

4. **What is your *brand*?** If you have to list it in only a few words, what would your words be?

5. After completing number four, you should be able to determine other words that fit into your branding to build your library of hashtags. ***Hashtags* are *keywords*** that people can use to find you easier. Think of hashtags like mini search engines. So if you do psychic readings, then you may want a hashtag of #psychicreading, #psychicmedium, or #intuition

You'll want to think about the focus of your photos. Not all photos are created equal, and not all of your photos need to be about the same thing. You want to create a feeling of relevance by meeting the needs and expectations of your followers.

If you want to focus on a spiritual lifestyle, for example, you may decide to post pictures about angels, crystals, or the many signs and symbols received from Spirit. Perhaps you want to share positive affirmations or photos that represent the healing effects of a session. Using photos that revolve around your mission statement and theme will help draw the right followers to your social media platform.

Instagram offers many filters. If you utilize them, be consistent in order to hone your branding. Finding ways to tie your content together will give it a feeling of added value to your potential clients.

YouTube

There are several ways to get your message out to the public. If you aren't too camera shy, creating videos on YouTube may be a great platform for you to explore. YouTube can give you the opportunity to showcase your work to the public. Video is a wonderful avenue to utilize if you plan on teaching or want the public to see your work if they haven't previously had a session with you.

With over 1 billion (yes, that's a B) viewers, YouTube has an audience of about one-third of the entire population using the internet – a massive potential audience from which you can draw! Furthermore, as the second-largest search engine, it can greatly assist you with developing and expanding your online presence when used properly.

Just remember you can't please everyone. With that being said, you may want to start off by only allowing "approved" comments. When you upload a video, you can select this option in the advanced settings. This will at least give you the opportunity to a view a comment prior to it being publicized. Also, when you start out, ask friends, family, and clients to help support your channel by subscribing. You may even want to consider a contest that entices clients to subscribe by offering a discount or special on a future session.

When creating videos, quality is king. You don't have to hire a personal videographer each time, but do put some thought into the final product. Create a video that adds value to the community. Small details like keeping the camera steady and using high-quality video and sound will bring a level of professionalism to your work. Professionalism helps create trust. Creating trust results in repeat clients.

Hootsuite 🦉 **Hootsuite**™

Hootsuite is basically a social media management tool. It will help you save time by allowing you to create posts for Facebook, Twitter, Google +, WordPress, and other social media platforms at once. You can create one post and schedule it to post to all of your social media accounts.

The positive side? Hootsuite helps you streamline your posts and make social media marketing less time-consuming. The downside? If you are in the spiritual business, you are in the business of personal connection. When reviewing the previous chapters, you can see how the different social media platforms utilize and focus on different attributes and messages.

For instance, Instagram is going to be the go-to place for posting your photos. Twitter will be your short status blog platform, while Facebook will help others discover more about you or your upcoming events. Now, each platform can do all of the above, but it's almost like knowing each one's personality and catering to its followers' needs and desires.

With Hootsuite, it seems inevitable that some of that personal touch will be lost, but if you can find a way to make each post unique to the platform, it can be a major player on your team!

Hashtags

You may be wondering why a pound sign is now called a #hashtag. A hashtag is a type of keyword or keyword phrase originally established by Twitter back in 2007; however, many of the major social media platforms now utilize them. Think of a hashtag as a mini google search. If you use the # sign before a word, it will automatically search all public posts for that keyword. The trick is to make your posts public and use your hashtag strategically.

Here are a few of the major keys in using your #hashtag to the max!

1. LESS IS MORE:

It's important to not use excessive hashtags in a post. If you use one or two, that's significant enough to have an impact and get your point across. No need for ten of them. This will turn followers off as it will come across more sales pitch than authentic. You don't want to dilute the importance of what you are trying to say in a post. In fact, studies show that your engagements will drop the more hashtags you use.

2. CREATE TARGETS:

Short and to the point. Keeping your hashtags shorter will help people absorb the meaning and keyword behind the hashtag. You may want to try #psychicmoon vs. something like #psychicmoonphasesforhoriscope

3. COMBINE WORDS:

The hashtag needs to be listed as one word. This is the case even if you are tying two words together like psychic and moon. If you use #psychic moon, the link will be broken, and only #psychic would be published as the hashtag with the post. By using #psychicmoon, you keep it as one unique searchable engine.

4. MAKE IT UNIQUE:

Make your tags unique. Allow your branding to shine through so that you stand out. #psychicsrock

5. ADVERTISE:

Use a #hashtag to announce an event. Let's say you are doing a live event for charity. The name of the event is Reiki Rescue. So use a hashtag #reikirescue in your post. This will help anyone who may have heard of the event but not have a direct link find it in social media searches.

6. **BE RELEVANT:**

Be sure to use hashtags that are relevant to what you are posting about. You don't want to post for a healing session and use a hashtag #needadrink

"Social media now gives you the power to connect directly with people that love what you create. You can make what you're passionate about and do what you love and like-minded people will find you. The way to stand out is to follow that passion and create because it drives you, not because you're trying to find some audience or grow your numbers. Anything else won't resonate because the lack of genuineness will show through and you'll also spend your time struggling to do something you don't actually enjoy. If you love what you're doing, you will stand out and your niche will find you."

-**Ali Spagnola**, *Musician*
Social Media Guru

Chapter *15*

Reviewing with Yelp!

Yelp is an online business directory that allows patrons to publish reviews regarding their personal experience with a business. The patron can leave between 1 star and 5 stars (with 5 being the best) and provide a detailed account of their experience. This can be a blessing and a curse – especially in the spiritual business where clients may have differing perceptions of their session.

In some instances, a client who has had an incredible session will leave a 5-star review.

However, in other cases, a client may not have been ready to hear the information they were given. This may result in a negative review, triggered by an emotional response or by the fact that they simply did not resonate with the information.

Before signing up for a Yelp account, it's best to build your experience and client base. Give yourself some time to feel comfortable with your practice. When you are first starting out, find acquaintances or friends willing to leave a review after their session. This way you are starting with those who already support your spiritual endeavors.

Yelp can be a great resource for potential clients to find you since the highest-rated service-providers will show up in search engines without paying for the Yelp advertising. If you can build positive, 5-star reviews, you will see your business grow.

Yelp has a filtering system, which means it can hide positive reviews. Many factors come into play here: it may be that the person who left the review was not previously active on Yelp or had posted only a few reviews. If the review is too short, lacks detail, or features too much detail, it could also trigger the filter and end up hidden since Yelp is looking for informative reviews posted by active users. Additionally, Yelp may hide a review if it believes two users are attempting to promote each other. Complicated, right? Well, look on the bright side: Yelp may also a negative review of your services, which would be to your benefit.

The site also offers advertising packages that would put your business at the very top of a search with the word AD next to it. It some instances, this is effective, but organic positive reviews may provide better results. Why? They show prospective clients that people genuinely appreciated their experience enough to share it for free. It's not paid advertising.

If you happen to get a negative review, try not to stress about it. The first time or two it happens, it may hurt your feelings. You can reach out to the person to simply let them know you are sorry they were disappointed, but at the same time, you must understand you won't be able to make everyone happy. As a healer, we want everyone to have an incredible session, but since people are in different stages of their life path, we may not always be able to accomplish 100% satisfaction. Ultimately, having a few lower star reviews has shown to be helpful to a business. Prospective clients feel it gives it a more realistic assessment. So if you happen to get a less than perfect review, don't worry – simply trust in your work and let Spirit do the rest!

One of the best ways to counter a negative review is to inform new clients that they can find you on Yelp. This may encourage them to leave a good review for you. Per Yelp policy, you are not allowed to ask specifically for a "positive" review, but a general request for reviews is acceptable.

Additionally, the site allows you to share. You can take a positive review or two and post them on your other social media platforms. You can also add a Yelp badge to your website.

If someone leaves an inaccurate, negative review or someone who wasn't even a client posts one, you can report it to Yelp. They will investigate it to see if complies with their policy. If they agree with you, they will remove it. But, don't be the boy who cried wolf! If you report a negative review simply because you didn't like it, Yelp may permit it to stay as long as it is true to the recipient's experience and refrains from being harassing or inflammatory.

Yelp can be an incredibly useful tool for your business, but it's one that you want to ensure you are ready to launch in order to build it confidently. Using the right tools as the right time is one of the keys in building your successful spiritual business.

Hopefully, this section has shown you the importance and impact social media can have on creating a thriving practice. It takes time to build your various platforms within social media, so be patient with yourself. As the saying goes, *Rome wasn't built in a day*. Go for quality over quantity and build a brand people will remember. If your posts are too generic, they will get missed. Your first impressions are your most important; give it thought, work from your heart and allow it all to grow organically.

Chapter 16

Newsletters and Blogs

Publishing Newsletters

A newsletter is an informational publication that is distributed periodically; for example, once a month. It provides updates and helpful information or guidance to your subscribers. How do you build subscribers? Your client list is one excellent way to do it, as long as you have express permission from the client. You may also post a sign-up link on the home page of your website or social media profile.

Offering an incentive for registering to your newsletter enables you to keep your clientele up to date with your events and offerings. For example, you may offer a free session once a month as a drawing to those who sign up on your list. Or, if they sign up, they receive a link to a special article only available to your subscribers. Once they register, they get a link to that article, which contains valuable information. While it can revolve around any topic, select one that is universally appealing to all of your clients.

These days, there are several software programs to choose from, but MailChimp and Constant Contact are two of the most popular. While I recommend doing your research to determine which features will work best for you, both MailChimp and Constant Contact will help you create mailing lists, campaigns, and newsletters. MailChimp even allows for a certain amount of FREE subscribers until you hit a particular threshold and, consequently, must sign up for a pro account. However, it's a great way to get started without any out-of-pocket expense.

A word of caution: do not make your newsletter solely promotional. You want to add content that is valuable to the reader within each edition. Showcasing a variety of information combining events, specials, articles, highlights, quotes, etc. will engage your audience and pique interest. Find ways to be creative and unique with your newsletter. Also, keep it simple. Endless pages may turn off your readers so it's important to keep the information straight and consistent to retain the most loyal subscribers.

Include certain items the reader can rely on each month. Let's say it's *Lucy's Love Lessons*. This could be a short little advice blog containing three tips for relationships. In each publication, it offers unique tips from a different perspective, but always on the topic of love. Every month your readers will anxiously await the three tips you are offering them for free!

While a newsletter may not be first on your to-do list, having an awareness that it's within your business plan will help you develop your voice along the way as you build your spiritual business. When the time comes to publish the newsletter on a regular basis, you will have taken most of the other necessary steps. This will naturally lead to the point of creating your loyal clientele and opening up the space to invite potential new clients as well.

Becoming a Blogger

Blogs have become the new form of self-expression. From personal experience to expert tips, blogs span across every topic imaginable. What is a blog? A blog is a mini website or webpage that is similar to an online diary or journal. It provides a platform for you to express yourself freely. From sharing personal stories or experiences to delivering helpful information, blogs are ultimately an expression of you. The great advantage of a blog is that there are less "rules" so you have the freedom of self-expression.

Having a blog is a great way to connect to your followers. You can maintain a blog as a page on your website and schedule a time to update it. Just determine a time that works best and commit to it. Your followers will learn to anticipate the release date, and soon you will discover you have a dedicated following eagerly awaiting each weeks topic.

Writing a successful blog takes a bit of practice, perseverance, and precision, but with these FIVE helpful tips you'll be on the fast track to capturing a loyal audience

1. **FOCUS**

Since you can't please everyone, focus on your target audience. Creating your blog with your intended audience in mind will help you develop content that will resonate with them in a way that they feel you're personally talking to them.

2. **CREATE**

Your title might be the most important part of your blog. You want to draw your reader in with a title that is original and catchy, but easily understandable. Trying to get too creative may have the opposite effect. For instance, let's say you want to talk about *Three ways to connect with spirit*. For a reader who is looking to understand their connection, this title is simple enough and lets the reader know what they can expect. If you were to have a title such as *The many ways we can expand our spiritual energy to connect in an expansive way to the other side.* This would be too long and complex of a title to reel a reader in quickly. You want to strive for a title that is short, concise and catchy!

3. WRITE

Since blogs are web-based, you have to make them engaging and easy to read. This is accomplished by writing short and impactful sentences. Blogs are meant to make a statement so stay on point with your sentences and don't create distractions with too much grammar graffiti.

4. STRUCTURE

An engaging blog must be visually pleasing. Format it in such a way that it's easy for a reader to understand the points you are trying to make. You can accomplish this by separating sentences to make statements or utilizing organizational tools such as numbers, bullets, etc. to highlight you're the main points.

5. ANGLE

Writing a blog that is memorable requires a unique angle. Finding your individual voice within your blog is what will help set it apart. Don't be afraid to stand apart from the pack with your angle. In the end, it's your angle that stands out.

If you have a voice and a passion for writing, consider a newsletter, article or blog as an avenue to help you connect with your audience. Finding multiple ways to contribute to the public can provide valuable insight to those craving information and give you a platform for self-expression.

Chapter 17
Managing Media

Whether you are a guest on a program or the host of your very own show, there are several factors that will determine its success. In today's world, media has become a dominant player; having a clear understanding to all of the moving parts is imperative to achieving a positive outcome either as a guest or as a host.

Regardless of your spiritual gift, professionalism is absolutely critical. Always bring your "A" game to any appearance. Knowing the proper questions to ask prior to the engagement and understanding how to respond to various situations will help you tremendously in achieving success!

Guest of Honor

Being invited to be a guest on a show is quite an honor. It demonstrates you have a presence and is a reflection that your gift is being noticed by others. When agreeing to be a guest on another's program, it's essential to be prepared. Having the most accurate information and show details will help to create a positive outcome.

Here's a list of recommended questions to ask before agreeing to be a guest on a program.

1. CONCEPT

What is show concept?

You may be able to research this on your own prior to asking the producer. You would hate to come across as not knowing of a show that's a top ten hit on iHeart radio! If you are unable to locate the show's description, then go ahead and ask so that you can determine if it's a good fit for you and your brand.

2. TOPIC

What is the topic of the episode?

Inquire on the angle of the episode prior to agreeing to it. Being comfortable with the angle or episode subject matter is important to ensure that you are in alignment with the purpose and perspective.

3. **FORMAT**

What is the format of the show? Is it a podcast, radio show, video series, television program?

Knowing the format beforehand allows you to prepare specifically for that particular medium. Sometimes a show may be a combination of configurations. For instance, some podcasts combine video, audio and live streaming simultaneously. When you are aware of the particular format, you will then have the opportunity to plan accordingly. If connecting via a live stream broadcast, you will want to be camera-ready.

4. **EXPECTATIONS**

Will you be doing demonstrations of your work?

Understanding the expectations pertaining to your show appearance will serve as a great benefit when setting your intentions. You don't want to be caught off guard by assuming you are doing a straightforward interview, only to discover they were expecting you to take live callers! Knowing what to expect helps you focus and attain a state of clarity so that you can deliver an outcome that is impactful and memorable.

Now that you have the program details, you can determine if the show is the right fit for you. Don't be afraid to decline the invite if it is not well-suited to your vision. You have a choice in how you work with your gift; honoring the integrity of your work should always supersede any potential prospect. Staying true to your most genuine and authentic self can only prevail with Spirit providing a plethora of future opportunities.

Agreeing to the Appearance

After contemplating the aforementioned questions, you agree to the appearance. *Now what*? First and foremost, give yourself a pat on the back and take a moment to appreciate the opportunity! You may experience nervousness, but that is only natural. Focus on being the professional.

Here are some vital keys to becoming a guest who is in demand:

1. CONFIRM DETAILS

Once you agree to an engagement, confirm, in writing, the details of the guest spot. Reaffirming the date, time, and format of the show will avoid any potential miscommunication. You never want to show up three hours late because you were on a different time zone! Once you've confirmed the details, put them in your calendar and set a reminder. Prior to the show, confirm any necessary log-in information. If your engagement is on Skype, Blog Talk Radio, or any other format, they may request that you connect to the studio prior to going live on air. Testing the login and the connection beforehand will help the show get off to a good start!

2. BE ON TIME

Most shows have a specific start time, which is usually inflexible. Being on time is critical because it's unprofessional to leave the producer or host in disarray trying to figure out how to fill the time until you arrive. If you live in a place that's notorious for heavy traffic or rely on public transportation, incorporate those factors into your planning. If you rely on outside help such as babysitters or pet sitters, give them an earlier time for arrival. Planning ahead will not only ease the stress if something should go wrong; it will also provide you with a sense of fortitude that you are ready for the opportunity.

3. **BE POLITE**

The importance of being polite cannot be stressed enough. Regardless if you are interacting with the receptionist, engineer, producer, or host; take the time to greet everyone with a smile. Always be courteous and respectful. This may seem obvious, but under pressure, we can sometimes be less patient. Treating everyone you meet with kindness will be remembered. You certainly don't want to leave an impression of being rude. It's surprising how much input the staff has on a show!

4. **MINIMIZE MOVEMENT**

Sound travels and sometimes our mannerisms are grand: we may talk with our hands or manifest our nervousness by making tapping, smacking or cracking sounds. Minimizing movement will surely be appreciated by the sound engineer. Avoid anything that could be a potential distraction to the show quality and your service to Spirit. Abstain from cracking your knuckles, smacking your lips, or tapping your microphone.

If demonstrating your gifts live on stage or on camera, your movements are all the more crucial. When provided a microphone, hold it firmly and speak into it directly. Despite your inner child, please refrain from casting it about like a magic wand! Be conscious of any excessive pacing. When working with energy, there may be a natural tendency to move back and forth, but for audience members, this can get quite distracting and make you appear nervous. Additionally, if you are working on camera, you want to always stay within the frame. Lastly, for on-camera appearances, ask the producers for your "marks." Sometimes indicated by tape on the floor, they represent the geographical area necessary to remain within the camera shot.

All of these may seem like minor infractions, but you would be amazed at how they translate on air.

5. SILENCE SOUNDS

It may sound obvious, but the ringing of a cell phone can be quite disturbing on a program. Prior to going on air, take a moment to silence your cell phone. Switching your phone to *Do Not Disturb* or *Airplane Mode* will avoid any extra jingles during the broadcast! There's always the giggle that God is calling, but avoiding the situation altogether is the most professional route to go.

An Ethernet or hard-wired connection is recommended to maintain a strong connection when doing any show via Skype. Wi-Fi connections tend to be temperamental and the having the call drop midway through the interview would be nothing short of embarrassing. Additionally, using headphones and muting your computer speakers will eliminate annoying feedback and provide the best audio quality experience for the listener.

If you wear jewelry, be mindful if it's clinking. It might be best to remove any jewelry that creates a sound upon movement. With the sophistication of recording devices, studios are quite sensitive to sound. Whether you are in a recording studio for a TV program, podcast or radio show, remembering to silence your external sounds shows that you are a true professional.

6. DRESSING THE PART

It's essential to dress the part when provided the opportunity to work in front of a camera or audience. You don't want to risk appearing unprofessional because you forgot to attend to a few minor details.

   ✓ **ATTIRE:** There cannot be enough emphasis placed on dressing the part. Learning the venue prior to your appearance so that you may dress appropriately is critical. How you would dress in a spiritual church vs. a reality TV program are drastically different. You always want to be respectful of the environment, culture and customs of your host. When in doubt, choose the more conservative approach and always keep a spare change of clothing in your car or bag in the event you suffer a mishap such as a spill or tear.

✓ **SWEAT:** As the saying goes *"never let them see you sweat"*. When working with Spirit, it's natural for your vibration to rise. You may also be feeling nervous. With these factors, you may sweat more than normal. However, it can be embarrassing if someone lifts their arms and exposes large sweat marks under their armpits. Finding a deodorant that helps protect against wetness or wearing an additional layer, such as an undershirt, can help prevent this from occurring and allow you to raise your arms confidently.

✓ **STRAPS:** Being mindful of your bra straps with your garment is an important consideration. You want to appear professional and put together when working. Having your colored bra strap sticking out from under your shirt, may not give the best impression to your audience. Doing a trial run with your clothing prior to an engagement gives you time to discover any potential wardrobe malfunctions.

✓ **HEELS:** If you choose to wear heels for an event, take a moment to walk in them on various types of floors. Some heels can be quite noisy, and if you are moving back and forth, they can become extremely distracting. There are rubber pads that can be placed on the bottom of shoes to help lessen the impact and reduce the sound.You want the audience to focus on you, not your shoes.

7. HAVE FUN

The most important aspect of agreeing to be a guest on any show is giving you permission to have fun! Of course, you may experience nervousness, but don't allow that to overshadow *WHY* you are doing this work! You are passionate about your role in creating healing for others, so make that your top priority. When you are relaxed, it will translate as being confident – and what better way to show you are a true professional than to exude confidence in your craft.

Many light-workers are driven to the spotlight for various reasons. Hold true to your highest purpose. No need to feel as if you need fame to make a change in the world. Work passionately and authentically. Allow Spirit to open the pathways for you to enter, but don't ever believe your worth is wrapped up in a green room. Being a guest on a program can be an enlightening and invaluable experience, but is never one that should dictate your self-worth.

Host with the Most

From high-definition video to streaming and Skype, there are countless choices to make when it comes to creating a show. Not everyone is cut out for the dedication of a media platform, but if you are committed, it could be a fun and creative way to get your message out there. Creating a show takes planning; investing time in developing a strategy will help eliminate failure.

There are many considerations to starting your own show. You have to consider the *Who, What, When, Where, Why and How* in order to build a successful framework. *What is your message? Who is your audience? How is your program unique? Where will you broadcast?*

WHO is your audience?

Examine who will be your target audience. Who is your message intended for? Do you have a desire to focus on investigative or medical intuition? Is it about solving cold cases or delivering heart-warming messages of healing and hope from the Afterlife? Perhaps it's about pet communication or paranormal investigation? When you recognize your audience, you can then develop your angle.

WHAT is your Angle?

Establish your angle. What will your perspective be for the show? Knowing your approach will help you determine what is needed to produce your concept. When you formulate your angle, you can then factor in the needs of your audience. Determining what differentiates your concept from other shows currently out there will help you devise your overall approach.

WHEN will it Air?

Your target audience will dictate the best time to air the program. Knowing the general habits of your audience and when they are most apt to tune into your show is key in creating a successful production. Start by looking at the type of clients you are booking for private sessions. Where are they geographically located? What is their approximate age range? What service do they seek most from you? Answering these questions will assist you in honing in on your target audience.

WHERE will you Broadcast?

Deciding on your platform depends on what you want to achieve with your show and budget. There are innumerable options and resources available for those who have a desire to host their own show. From Blog Talk Radio to other internet-based programming, you can relax in knowing there is a fit for you. Other alternatives include Skype, in-studio, podcast and of course radio. Some companies even offer a combination of elements – think of it as a la carte programming.

If you are camera shy and don't feel like having the world look at you, an audio program would be better suited to your preferences. Do you want to take callers? Have in-studio guests? Be available around the world? These are all questions to consider before starting your broadcast media adventure.

WHY are you Inspired?

Making the decision to create a show is only the start, but you will have to dig deep to know WHY you are feeling driven to have a show. Finding your deeper sense of purpose will carry you through the points when you may feel like giving up if success isn't immediate. Being connected to your inner drive, purpose and calling for a program will help to keep you motivated when you may lack enthusiasm. Sometimes it will take self-discipline, but it's so much easier when you have a strong sense of purpose behind it.

HOW will it be Different?

Sit and contemplate HOW your show will differentiate itself from others. In today's age of impulse and impatience, finding a way to attract and maintain a following is imperative to success. Doing the same old formats already in existence simply won't work. Start by looking inward. If you are part of the show, ask yourself *How you are different*? Hopefully, you examined this in the beginning when you initially started the book. Bringing your personality forward is definitely a step in the right direction because there is only ONE you. Finding a way to be creative, fresh, and interesting can mean a great deal of work, but it will be well worth the effort when you connect to your audience in the way you always envisioned.

"Guesting and hosting are two very different jobs with differing priorities. Content is what most guests are concerned with and that should remain a priority. Be concise and clear; be certain you have something to say. But most are not aware that as guest your primary job is to assist in making a show as good as possible. This includes maintaining the rhythm and energy of that particular program. You want to help make viewers or listeners stop and stay with a program. A component of that job should be to help the host and enhance his or her job. In other words, help make the host look good. Also be clear on the expectations of the segment producer and aim to make that person look as good as possible for having selected you for the show. Other than these considerations just how up with a good attitude, dress appropriately, be available when called, show up on time, and you will be asked back."

-**Dr. Drew Pinsky**, *host of* 'This Life with Dr. Drew and Bob Forrest' *and longtime host of KROQ's 'Loveline'*

Part **5**:

TERMS AND CONDITIONS

Chapter 18

Disclosing Your Disclaimer

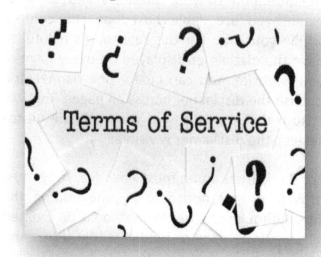

A disclaimer is a statement that defines in very clear terms the intentions, limitations, and obligations of your services. It is used to limit risk and inform any potential client to the scope of your practice. This is particularly important in an industry in which clients may rely on your work for specific results. Having precise and unequivocal language in your disclaimer may restrict what claims may be made against you by those who have utilized your services.

A court of law will consider the language and the placement of the disclaimer to determine the intention of your business and to what extent you are liable based on the content within your site. For this reason, it's helpful to have the disclaimer displayed on every page of your website. You can create one banner and publish the disclaimer across all pages. This will ensure that regardless of what tab the visitor selects, the disclaimer is visible.

For disclaimers to be most effective, they must provide proper notice to anyone visiting the site. Although the disclaimer could be created as a separate page or hidden within terms and conditions, the best practice is to have it visible and prominently placed on your website. Since you are in the service industry, you want to consider language that informs a visitor that you are not a substitute for medical, emotional or legal counsel.

Below is a sample DISCLAIMER:

This service and the use of this website is for entertainment purposes only and is intended for and may only be used by adults 18 years of age or older. By your use of this website, you confirm that you are at least 18 years old. This website and its creators make no representations or warranties, either express or implied, concerning the accuracy, relevancy, or quality of information provided. We do not assume and hereby disclaim any liability to any person or entity for any loss or damages (including, without limitation, physical, medical, mental, financial, special, indirect, incidental or consequential) caused with regard to any information and/or any suggestion(s) or advice provided to you through this service, or as a result of your use of this service. The readings and/or information provided are for entertainment purposes only, and if you choose to rely on them, you specifically agree to do so at your own risk assuming full responsibility. What you decide to do with the information given to you, including any actions you take, is your own personal responsibility and choice. We reserve the right to refuse service to anyone and/or to discontinue this website at any time. This service is not intended to address any medical, physical, mental, emotional, financial and/ or legal issues. It is for entertainment purposes only. You should, therefore, consult a medical care, mental health care, financial specialist and/or legal professional for any medical, physical, mental, emotional, financial and/or legal issues that need professional attention.

Medical Disclaimer

Unless you are a licensed physician, refrain from dispensing medical diagnosis and/or treatment, or prescribing medication. This could be misconstrued as providing claim of unauthorized practice of medicine or medical negligence. If a client tells you about their symptoms, suggest that they see a medical professional and inform them that you are not licensed to diagnose.

Consult with your legal counsel to determine if your business does fall within the guidelines of a "complementary health care provider." Some states have enacted laws that have created a bit of freedom with alternative medicine. For instance, in California, Senate Bill SB577 was signed into law by Governor Davis on September 23, 2002, and became effective on January 1, 2003. Upon signing the law, Gov. Davis stated SB577 "will ease access to alternative and complementary health care options for all Californians."

CLIENT DISCLAIMER

I_____ understand that I am responsible for my health and my health choices and that, per Federal and State Law, only a medical doctor is able to make any claims to diagnose, treat, prevent, or cure disease, prescribe prescription drugs and/or adjust my dosage of prescription drugs.

I understand that all information and all correspondence verbally, via email, brochure, letter or otherwise does in no way make any claims to diagnose, treat, prevent or cure me of any aliment, affliction, suffering, or disease that I have had, currently have or will have in the future. Additionally, I understand that if I rely on any additional information related to financial decisions, relationships or otherwise, I do so at my own risk.

I therefore, release _____, its employees, officers, owners and representatives from any past, present, or future health, financial or other liability issues that I may have. I also acknowledge that I am seeking services or products of my own free will and choice and that I was not, nor have been, forced, mislead or coerced by any statement made verbally or in writing. I understand that it is the intention of this therapy that a person is supported as a whole person for optimizing wholeness and success. I understand I will not be prescribed any prescription medications with these services, however I am encouraged to provide open communication between _____ and any of my doctors and/or practitioners I am currently working with.

I understand that _____ will not provide a diagnosis and by law cannot provide a diagnosis. I also understand that it is important that I know what is going on with my own body so I confirm that I have received a medical diagnosis or am under the care of a licensed physician to receive a medical diagnosis. _____ (initial).

Additionally:

* I understand that no physician-patient relationship is established through participation in energy reading and/or my relationship with _____.
* I understand that this work is not psychotherapy.
* I understand that information regarding the energy of the body and/or _____ is provided for educational purposes and that there is no guarantee of monies to be made or successes as no one is able to guarantee money and/or success.
* I understand that this work is not medical diagnosis, medical treatment or medical advice; therefore I will not be provided prescription, treatment, diagnoses, cure or psychotherapy.
* I understand that I will be billed for the duration of the appointment, not for the amount of time scheduled.
* I understand that I am the person who has the most influence over the energy of my body and that any services I receive is to assist me with working with my own energy.
* Some appointments may be helpful to record for repeated listening, and some may not. Please initial if you are open to having your appointment recorded exclusively for your listening only. _____

I clearly understand and agree that all services rendered to me are charged directly to me, and that I am personally responsible for payment which is due at the time of service.

I have read, understand and fully agree to the above information:

Name (please print neatly): _____

Signature:_____Date:_____

Parent or Guardian Signature (if under 18): _____

www.   tel:

In a nutshell, states and countries have varying laws pertaining to healthcare and healthcare-related services. Review your practice with your attorney to ensure you are in compliance with the governing laws of your area.

Here is the link to read the senate bill in its entirety:
ftp://www.leginfo.ca.gov/pub/01-02/bill/sen/sb_0551-0600/sb_577_bill_20020923_chaptered.html

Although a disclaimer cannot guarantee against legal action, it can provide for clear communication regarding your intent and notify clients that they are personally responsible for their actions.

It is highly recommended to seek the services of a professional lawyer to assist with the necessary language required for your specific practice. Since language and intention are factors considered by a court, it is an invaluable investment in building your spiritual business.

Requiring a client to sign a disclaimer prior to rendering services is an additional safety measure that helps protect the practitioner.

Below is a sample Client Disclaimer for your use.

Feel free to download it here:
http://colbyrebel.com/client-disclaimer/

"Those who learn to bring the fire and love of inspiration into the physical world are unstoppable agents of positive change."

-**Robert Montano**, *Legal, Business & Spiritual Adviser*

Chapter 19

Company Policies

A policy that explicitly states the terms and conditions of appointments upon which cancellations are acceptable is an essential component to your business.

By prominently displaying a cancellation policy on your website, one that a client can see and agree to prior to booking a session, you can avoid potential misunderstandings. Without a clearly defined policy, a client could cancel or not show up for an appointment without prior notification, then request a refund. This would oblige you to return their payment since you did not clarify the terms prior to the booking.

Being straightforward about your cancellation policy will provide the necessary guidelines and inform potential clients of the company's terms and conditions.

In the event of a last-minute cancellation, you will then have the discretion of whether to issue a refund or a credit, or inform the client they are not due a refund based upon the company policy. Your cancellation policy should include the details that would allow the cancellation to be valid. This may be the amount of notice needed prior to the appointment and the manner in which they need to provide the notice. *Does it need to be in writing? Can they simply leave a message?* Requiring written communication will give you a trackable resource and avoid any *"Well, I left you a message, you didn't get it?"* excuses.

The more you can avoid miscommunication in regard to your company's terms and conditions, the more you will alleviate any stress related to policies – which will allow you to focus on what you do best, helping clients!

Refund Policy

A refund policy is exactly what it sounds like: a policy that establishes the guidelines for which a refund would be feasible and permissible. Making your refund policy openly visible on your website prior to permitting the client to book a session will aid in demonstrating full disclosure. Requiring a client to acknowledge that they have read and understand the terms and conditions of the policy prior to booking creates an additional safeguard.

Ultimately, we want a satisfied and happy client because happy clients make for great referrals! They become our biggest advocates, and since you are in the business of customer relations, you always want to do your absolute best to ensure their satisfaction. However, every now and again, you may encounter someone who simply isn't happy with the service. The refund policy outlines the company protocol and informs the client whether or not they are within their rights to receive a refund. As with any practice, you may have to occasionally use discernment to approve any exceptions to the policy, but having one in place will at least provide you with that option.

Consider the conditions in which you would offer a refund. *If they cancel last minute? Do you guarantee results? What if they simply didn't feel as if they connected? Would you set a time limit within the start of the session to determine if the connection?* Knowing your conditions will help you customize your policy to fit both your needs and those of the client.

A refund policy may not necessarily be a legal requirement in your area, but being proactive in avoiding miscommunication by clearly stating the terms and conditions is recommended.

Consult with your legal counsel to determine if there are specific laws in your area that require additional compliance.

Client Intake Form

An intake form may be of assistance in understanding your clients' needs, objectives, and overall goals. They can also be utilized as a blueprint in creating a plan of action for your client and allows for clear communication regarding your intent. Additionally, it expresses your terms in working with a client and what they can anticipate from that session.

Requiring a client to complete a client intake prior to rendering services is a measure that helps provide the practitioner with necessary information to best assist the client.

Here is a sample client intake form. You may also download the form here:
http://colbyrebel.com/client-intake-form-sample/

Leap of Faith

INTAKE FORM

PERSONAL: Date: _____

Full Name:_____

Address: _____

Phone #: Home (_____)_____   Cell: (_____)_____

Email Address: _____

Gender: Male   Female   Birth date: Age: _____

Height:_____   Approx. Weight: _____

Marital Status: Married   Single   Divorced   Widowed

Name of Spouse, Parent, or Guardian: _____

EMERGENCY CONTACT INFORMATION:

Name:_____Phone: _____

Address: _____

Relationship: _____

Please Sign and Return: You are welcome to fill out as much or as little of the following information as you like, though more information can be more helpful to assist you in achieving your goals.

GOALS:

Please describe in as much detail as possible what you main goals are in working together, in order of importance. Please be as specific as possible and include any blocks or trauma you feel you may be having whether they be business, relationship, health, emotional or other. Use additional paper if needed.

_____

_____

_____

_____

_____

_____

_____

A practitioner may want to extend this section and ask more detailed questions relating to the clients background, past successes and challenges, health and/or financial history, career, priorities, expectations etc. tailored to the specific needs of the treatment protocol.

The terms of our working together shall be as follows:

I. Appointments and Assignment

This section is optional but may be included to describe the specifics of working together. It is best used if there is a certain set time period to work together (say one a week for 6 months) or if there are details to the relationships. Such things may include, a) in person versus phone consultations, b) email support or no and if so under what terms, c) homework for the client and the expectations associated with it, d) monthly retainers and/or e) and special payment arrangements (for example, payment being a percentage of a project instead of a set rate etc.).

In the context of a more formal coaching or other arrangement, the following sections may also want to be included.

II. Confidentiality

The techniques, tools, processes written materials, homework and all other things, concepts and/or ideas I use with my coaching clients and otherwise ("Confidential Information") are based on my many years of experience and are individually tailored to meet your specific needs.   They are proprietary and strictly confidential and though I certainly want you to utilize them to the fullest in the context of our coaching relationship, you are not permitted to share, use or distribute them in any way without my express written permission.

III. Miscellaneous

    a. This document shall be interpreted pursuant to the laws of the State of _____and _____ shall have exclusive jurisdiction and venue for any and all issues between the parties.

    b. You have right to enter this coaching relationship and do so in abidance with all laws, rules and regulations.

    c. This agreement may not be assigned or transferred without the express written consent of the other party.

    d. Each party agrees that unauthorized disclosure of the Confidential Information may irreparably damage the other party. Such damages cannot be fully compensated by money damages. Therefore, each party agrees that relief for such disclosure may be sought in equity, for which no bond will be required.

I have read, understand and fully agree to the above information:

Name (please print neatly): _____

Signature:_____Date:_____

Parent or Guardian Signature (if under 18): _____

Chapter 20
Ethics and Integrity

in·teg·ri·ty
in'tegrədē/the quality of being honest and having strong moral principles; moral uprightness.

Ethics and Integrity may be difficult to define because our personal experience and perception comprise our overall belief system. In an industry constantly plagued by allegations of fraud and charlatans, the public is craving legitimacy. People *want* to believe, and as a healer in the new world, this is your opportunity to elevate the standard. By accepting responsibility for your part in revolutionizing the perception of the metaphysical industry, you can contribute to creating a shift that reveres light-workers with the same level of credibility and respect as doctors, teachers, accountants, scientists, and lawyers.

How many times have you seen a doctor walking around a grocery store giving a diagnosis to the customer in the produce aisle? Probably not too many, right? Avoid the temptation of giving readings or healings to random strangers you meet in public. It's these practices that have triggered apprehension among the public. Some of you may be thinking *"but I can't help it, Spirit won't leave me alone."* Practicing as a professional is having the control to "turn it off" when you're not working in that professional capacity. Through discipline and training, you will find that you do have the ability to refrain from delivering a message.

In an evolving world of enlightenment, you may not be able to convert the skeptic, but your actions can reflect a level of professionalism resulting in a heightened respect for the industry as a whole.

Create a safe haven for clients to trust and surrender. People will entrust you with their deepest fears, secrets, and desires; please take this honor as a privilege and provide them with a protective and safe environment conducive for healing.

Delivering Messages

Delivering a message can be a complicated endeavor at times, especially when there is a tragedy and sudden loss surrounding the loved one. It is imperative to handle the message with integrity. The client will carry what you say about their loved one with them **forever**. They will cling to your words; from their perspective, it's the last bit they have of their beloved. There is an obligation to "give what you get" and be the true "medium" of Spirit, but it can be handled with grace and compassion.

Imagine if someone told you that your loved was "stuck" and unable to transition fully to the other side and that it was your responsibility to help them.

Can you fathom what that would feel like?

There's story from a client who had gone to a pet communicator after her precious "Trixi" had passed away. The pet medium told the client that Trixi was "stuck in a green jelly" and that the client "had to figure out what the dog needed" so that it could fully transition. This is a person who loved her dog like a child. She rescued, pampered and spent thousands of dollars on medical treatment to give this fur-baby the best quality of life possible. Words can traumatize and scar a client. Being mindful of our words and messages can take a session from the most traumatizing to the most healing simply by being caring and compassion in how the message is delivered.

Avoid Gossip

Throughout your career, you will encounter many other healers. There are guaranteed to be some that you prefer over others, but remember to always be respectful to all. Maintaining strong relationships is vital to a successful business. If you hear whispers among colleagues regarding another light-worker, simply refrain from engaging. When in doubt, ask yourself what would you be willing to say to the person directly? What if they could hear your conversation? Focus on building connections with others so that you have a community to collaborate with and shy away from words or actions that don't come from your highest self.

When in doubt, remember The Four Agreements by *Don Miguel Ruiz*.

The Four Agreements:

1. Be impeccable with your word.
2. Don't take anything personally.
3. Don't make assumptions.
4. Always do your best.

*– **Miguel Ruiz**, The Four Agreements: A Practical Guide to Personal Freedom*

Upholding Boundaries

Upholding boundaries and exercising ethics is another element. Be cautious of becoming too intimate with a client. If a close relationship develops, ask yourself if you are truly working for the person's "highest good" and in the name of Spirit. Working as a professional requires understanding your boundaries and limits as a light-worker. If you choose to continue a personal relationship, consider referring them to another light-worker for future professional sessions.

This holds true for friendships as well. If you know every little detail of a dear friend's life, withhold the temptation to read for them. We may all need a little insight or advice here or there from our friends – that's normal, but refrain from engaging in full sessions. There's a conflict of interest and with any solid professional, we want to avoid crossing that boundary at all times. There is an ethical duty in this work, and we must make an oath to ourselves and Spirit to work responsibly.

Avoiding Substances

Don't work under the influence of alcohol or other substances. You wouldn't want a doctor performing a surgery while intoxicated, so handle your own profession with equal standards. The same holds true for a client. If they arrive for an appointment intoxicated or under the influence of drugs or other substances, refrain from continuing the session. Their judgment is impaired, which goes back to creating a safe and protective environment.

Diagnosis

As previously stated in Chapter 18, avoid dispensing medical diagnosis, treatment or prescribe medication unless you are legally authorized in your area.

Setting Limits

Set a limit as to how many times you agree to see a client within a particular time period. Some clients can become addicted to healing, guidance, and readings; it's up to you to set the boundaries. If you state the terms and include them within the policy on your website, you will always have something to refer back to should you need to inform a client you are unable to work them. You can also explain that time is necessary for the energy to manifest; therefore, you will see them again within *X* amount of months.

Research

Never research a client prior to a session. It may be easy to get wrapped up in the stardom of a client or succumb to the pressure needing to be accurate, but trust your gift completely. If you don't get a name or every perfect fact, this is a GOOD thing! Trust what spirit gives to you. If you research, google or Facebook, etc. you are jeopardizing your reputation and dishonoring the integrity of spirit. Trust your gift and know that spirit will provide.

Say Please and Thank-You

Taking a moment to thank someone for their generosity and kindness can have far-reaching effects. It communicates that you are sincere, appreciative and grateful, and adds an element of professionalism. Over the past several years, the art of personal thank-you cards has been replaced with impersonal emails; taking the time to write and physically mail a thank you note takes your gratitude to a whole new level. One that is impactful and memorable. When building a business, we want to make an impact. Showing your genuine gratitude for those who have helped you along your path can set you apart from others and make a lasting impression. It's the small acts that can make all the difference.

Additionally, as an added benefit, thank-you cards are a great opportunity to reinforce your branding by simply having your name and logo printed directly on the cards.

Philosophy

When entering your practice, stay true to your own philosophy. There will be times when you feel tested and uncertain of your path; this is completely *normal*. Staying connected to your soul keeps you committed to your calling and guides you to always serve for the highest good.

Conclusion

Ready to take **YOUR** *Leap of Faith*?

Well, you made it to the end, but honestly, this is just your beginning! You now have everything you need to build your own successful spiritual business. This book is your roadmap. You are no longer on a scavenger hunt trying to find your way. It encompasses everything you need to know and takes you step-by-step through the process of breaking out into the world and making a positive impact with your gift.

We have covered all of the major areas that are vital in establishing yourself as a professional and a trusted business. By addressing these topics one-by-one, you have the luxury of seeing what it takes to stand out in the industry and shine brightly among the many other light-workers. Use this book to find your own unique path. Discover the ways that highlight your strengths and showcase your work with Spirit.

Embrace and love yourself in the way that Spirit sees you. Your contribution to the world of Spirit is invaluable. Committing to your purpose and staying on your course of action will become a beacon of light for clients who need you.

When you accomplish a task or reach a goal, share it with a friend or family member. Surround yourself with those who support your endeavor. Relish in your victories and learn from any setbacks. They are all part of the plan that Spirit has designed for you. This is your ride – roll down the windows and throw up your hands! Surrender to Spirit and watch how the Universe responds.

There will be times when you feel unsure and question your course. Whenever this happens, go back and ask yourself "what is my next step?" Each time you move beyond your comfort zone and trust in your calling, you will find the courage to push to the next level. Take the information and tips in this book and utilize them in a way that fits for you.

This is your time. Where do you want to go next on your journey? And are you going to take a step or are you going to take a Leap of Faith?

With Gratitude,

Colby

Weblink Resources

Chapter 5

Learn more about Bob Olsen's Best Psychic Directory
http://www.bestpsychicdirectory.com/phelp.html

Learn more about Best American Psychics:
www.bestamericanpsychics.com

To perform a name search in California visit:
http://kepler.sos.ca.gov

Chapter 8

A few popular booking systems to consider:
www.acuityscheduling.com
https://bookedin.com
http://www.vcita.com
http://www.supersaas.com
https://www.genbook.com
http://www.appointy.com
http://www.fullslate.com

Chapter 11

You can apply for an EIN directly online by visiting:
https://www.irs.gov/businesses/small-businesses-self-employed/apply-for-an-employer-identification-number-ein-online

Chapter 12

Gather more information on bookkeeping software by visiting:
http://quickbooks.intuit.com or http://www.quicken.com

To download form W-9:
https://www.irs.gov/pub/irs-pdf/fw9.pdf

To Download Expense Sheet:
http://colbyrebel.com/expensesheet/

Chapter 13

Office in home:
https://www.irs.gov/uac/about-publication-587

You can check IRS publication 463
https://www.irs.gov/pub/irs-pdf/p463.pdf

One site that offers mileage tracking is TripLog:
https://triplogmileage.com/IRS-Uber-tax-deduction.html

To learn more about self-employed business expenses:
https://www.irs.gov/businesses/small-businesses-self-employed/deducting-business-expenses

Chapter 14

To learn more about Facebook ad policies visit:
https://www.facebook.com/policies/ads/

YouTube Stat:
http://www.mushroomnetworks.com/infographics/youtube---the-2nd-largest-search-engine-infographic

Chapter 18

To read SB577:
ftp://www.leginfo.ca.gov/pub/01-02/bill/sen/sb_0551-0600/
sb_577_bill_20020923_chaptered.html

Download your client disclaimer form:
http://colbyrebel.com/client-disclaimer/

Chapter 19

Download your client intake form here:
http://colbyrebel.com/client-intake-form-sample/

Quotes– Contact Information

Shaun Briggs
"Bringing Ideas To Life"
Graphics I Websites I Branding
www.shaunbriggs.com

Jamie J. Cottage, CPA, CEO
Cottage & Associates, Inc.
Certified Public Accountants
8383 Wilshire Blvd, Suite 360
Beverly Hills, CA 90211
T: 323-275-4750
www.cottage-cpas.com

Lizzie Martell, Illustrator
Lizzie Martell Illustration
ArtistlDesignerlIllustrator
www.lizziemartell.com

Robert Montano, Legal, Business & Spiritual Adviser
T: 615.587.8811
E: RMontano8@yahoo.com

Allen H. Park, CPA, MBT
Apark Accountancy
T: 213.805.6590
www.aparkaccountancy.com

Shay Parker, Founder
Best American Psychics
www.bestamericanpsychics.com

Georgi Petrov, CEO & Lead Designer
Designroom1229 & Flyer Room
www.designroom1229.com

Dr. Drew Pinsky, Celebrity Physician
Host of Dr. Drew on HLN, This Life podcast,
former host of the nationally hit radio show Loveline
www.drdrew.com

Michael Roud, CEO
Michael Roud Photography
11223 Magnolia Blvd
North Hollywood, CA 91601
T: 818.506.4700
www.michaelroud.com

Ali Spagnola, Social Media Celebrity
Ali Spagnola
http://alispagnola.com

Wendy Wiseman, Owner
Pixels Digital Imaging
6907 ½ Melrose Ave.
Los Angeles, CA 90038
T: 323.954.1582
http://www.pixelsla.com

Further Reading

Brene' Brown Ph.D., *The Gifts of Imperfection*

Paulo Coelho, *The Alchemist*

Michael Hyatt, *Platform Get Noticed In A Busy World*

Gary Keller with Jay Papasan, *The One Thing*

Richard Nugent, *The 50 Secrets of Self-Confidence*

Don Miguel Ruiz, The Four Agreements: A Practical Guide to Personal Freedom (A Toltec Wisdom Book)

Gary Vaynerchuk, *JAB, JAB, JAB, RIGHT HOOK: How To Tell Your Story In A Noisy World*

Lisa Williams, *The Survival of the Soul* and *I Speak to Dead People Can You?*

Oprah Winfrey, *What I Know for Sure*

Disclosures

IRS Circular 230 Disclosure: To ensure compliance with requirements imposed by the Internal Revenue Service, we inform you that any U.S. tax advice contained in this communication (including attachments) is not intended to be used, and cannot be used, for the purpose of (i) avoiding penalties under the Internal Revenue Code or (ii) promoting, marketing, or recommending to another party any transaction or matter addressed herein.

About the Author

Colby is an international psychic medium, master spiritual teacher, radio host, author, and public speaker.

She has endured vigorous testing and is a *Certified* Master Spiritual Teacher of both psychic and mediumship development through the Lisa Williams International School of Spiritual Development in Los Angeles, California (LWISSD), having been personally invited to the program by world-renowned psychic medium Lisa Williams. Colby is a *Certified Spiritual Advisor,* ™ Advanced Psychic, and Advanced Medium through LWISSD. She has also studied at the acclaimed Arthur Findlay College in Stansted, England.

Prior to taking the Leap of Faith to build her own spiritual practice, Colby worked in public accounting and taxation for fourteen years. From 2010 to 2015, she served as a tax manager for a Los Angeles firm. She shares her experience and knowledge for the purpose of giving you the direction, inspiration, and tools you need to build your own successful spiritual business.

Colby hosts her popular show, *Colby Rebel Live* on UBN Radio and contributes to OM Times Magazine as a spotlight writer. She lives in Los Angeles, California where she owns and teaches from the Colby Rebel Spirit Center.

Contact Colby

To get the latest updates on
Leap of Faith:
HOW TO BUILD YOUR SPIRITUAL BUSINESS
www.colbyrebel.com

Colby is available for keynote speaking, consultation and seminars on the topic of building a successful spiritual business.

She also conducts workshops on spiritual development including: intuition, psychic and mediumship.

More ways to connect with Colby:

Email: **Info@colbyrebel.com**

Facebook: **www.facebook.com/PsychicRebel/**

Twitter: **twitter.com/PsychicRebel**

Instagram: **www.instagram.com/psychicrebel/**